INFLATION TARGETING AND POLICY RULES

The Case of Mexico, 2001–2012

INFLATION TARGETING AND POLICY RULES

The Case of Mexico, 2001–2012

Oscar Rodríguez Medina and Elías Alvarado Lagunas

APPLE ACADEMI PRESS

Apple Academic Press Inc. | Apple Academic Press Inc.
3333 Mistwell Crescent | 9 Spinnaker Way
Oakville, ON L6L 0A2 | Waretown, NJ 08758
Canada | USA

First issued in paperback 2021

Exclusive worldwide distribution by CRC Press, a member of Taylor & Francis Group
No claim to original U.S. Government works

ISBN 13: 978-1-77463-583-4 (pbk)
ISBN 13: 978-1-77188-268-2 (hbk)

Library and Archives Canada Cataloguing in Publication

Rodríguez Medina, Oscar, author
Inflation targeting and policy rules : the case of Mexico, 2001–2012 / Oscar Rodríguez Medina and Elías Alvarado Lagunas.

Includes bibliographical references and index.
Issued in print and electronic formats.
ISBN 978-1-77188-268-2 (hardcover).--ISBN 978-1-77188-472-3 (pdf)
1. Monetary policy--Mexico. 2. Inflation targeting--Mexico.
I. Alvarado Lagunas, Elías, author II. Title.

HG665.R63 2015   332.4'10972   C2015-906296-9   C2015-906297-7

Library of Congress Cataloging-in-Publication Data

Names: Rodrâiguez Medina, Oscar, author. | Alvarado Lagunas, Elâias, author.
Title: Inflation targeting and policy rules : the case of Mexico, 2001-2012 / Oscar Rodrâiguez Medina and Elâias Alvarado Lagunas.
Description: Toronto; New Jersey : Apple Academic Press, 2015. | Includes bibliographical references and index.
Identifiers: LCCN 2015034834 | ISBN 9781771882682 (alk. paper)
Subjects: LCSH: Inflation targeting--Mexico. | Anti-inflationary policies--Mexico.
Classification: LCC HG665 .R63 2015 | DDC 339.50972/090511--dc23
LC record available at http://lccn.loc.gov/2015034834

Apple Academic Press also publishes its books in a variety of electronic formats. Some content that ap-pears in print may not be available in electronic format. For information about Apple Academic Press products, visit our website at **www.appleacademicpress.com** and the CRC Press website at **www.crc-press.com**

ABOUT THE AUTHORS

Oscar Rodríguez Medina

Oscar Rodríguez Medina is a specialist in monetary and financial economics and holds a Master's degree in economics and bachelor of economics from the Universidad Nacional Autónoma de México (UNAM). He is also a PhD student in economics at the Instituto de Investigaciones Economicas in Mexico City. He has been a lecturer in the faculty of economics and a research assistant in the Instituto de Investigaciones Económicas (IIEc) of the UNAM. His particular area of research is monetary theory and policy.

Elías Alvarado Lagunas

Elías Alvarado Lagunas, PhD, is currently a lecturer and researcher with the Facultad de Contaduría Pública y Administración at the Universidad Autónoma de Nuevo León (UANL), Mexico. His areas of specialilzation include development economics and public management, as well as regional and local development. Dr. Lagunas received his social sciences PhD in sustainable development from the Universidad Autónoma de Nuevo León (UANL) and his Master's degree in industrial economy by the UANL. He is a member of Sistema Nacional de Investigadores (SNI).

CONTENTS

LIST OF ABBREVIATIONS

ADF	augmented Dickey–Fuller
BANXICO	Banco de México
CETES	Certificados de la Tesoreria de la Federación
DW	Durbin–Watson
ESCB	European System of Central Banks
EU	European Union
FED	Federal Reserve System
FOMC	Federal Open Market Committee
GDP	gross domestic product
IGAE	Indicador Global de la Actividad Económica
IIEc	Instituto de Investigaciones Económicas
INPC	National Index of Consumer Prices (Indice Nacional de Precios al Consumidor)
IMF	International Monetary Fund
INEGI	Instituto Nacional de Estadística y Geografía
IT	inflation-targeting approach
OLIR	optimal long-run inflation rate
OLS	ordinary least squares
PP	Phillips–Perron
SNI	Sistema Nacional de Investigadores
TIIE	Tasa de interés Interbancaria de equilibrio
UANL	Universidad Autónoma de Nuevo León
UNAM	Universidad Nacional Autónoma de México
VAR	vector autoregression

INTRODUCTION

The recent financial crisis in 2007 and the economic derivative initiated in 2008 are evidence that the world in which we live is inserted in a structure of constant volatility and uncertainty. This stochastic environment was the subject of several discussions between streams of economic thought and a constant search for a solution. The economic literature throughout its history has not been able to define the way in which they operate local, regional, national economies and the global economy. It has been unable to predict unexpected events that tend to be catastrophic to macro-level and micro-economic strata.

The main debate focuses, on the one hand, on the regulation of the economy, ranging from the appearance of commercial, institutional, exchange, capital, etc., as the leader axis that allows almost the complete elimination of the recurrent volatility which are subject to different variables and the different components of an economy. On the other hand is position that fully sympathizes with the liberalization of markets that the regulation aims to monitor. Such liberalization would certainly imply a process governed by the performance of supply and demand, which, in the best of cases, would behave "evenly".

However, both cases present aspects to consider: the first would cause concentrations of power that would undoubtedly be translated into the formation of monopolies that would mainly affect the final consumer for not very long periods. The second would involve a permanent random component in any aspect of a country's economy, which in the medium and long terms would cause a process of widespread loss of confidence of private agents who, in turn, would lead to the loss of the balance mentioned in advance.

A significant part of the previous discussion implies, therefore, that it is better use of any systematic behavior by authorities to clearly describe its actions to govern the performance of the economy, or deliberately react to short-term events; this means, if discretionary when it comes to implementing specific movement. The decision to opt for one or the other position depends on with what economic theory sympathetic managers implement economic policies. This is essential for developed countries but, obviously, is of vital importance for markets of unstable economies, such as developing and emerging countries.

Now, at the end of the years seventy joined the economic literature the concept called "rational expectations hypothesis", created in 1961 by John Muth. These times were characterized by the inability of the economic Keynesian policy of solving problems (stagflation), and it resumed to importance the use of monetary policy rather than the requirement of the economy as primary prosecutor. Thus, government's authorities turned again to look toward monetary policy, as it was up to before the great depression of 1929. However, economists such as Milton Friedman and Edmund Phelps had challenged the way which applied economic policy through the Phillips curve.

This analysis allowed the old Phillips curve expectations of Adaptive type to be incorporated which, subsequently, was associated with the concept of the natural rate of unemployment introduced in 1968 by Friedman. Then the hypothesis of rational expectations, embedded as a course, which should be understood as a methodology of modeling and not as a current or theory of economic thought, revolutionized the macroeconomic in the sense of modular discretionary countercyclical policies through presumably to agents capable of using the available range of information, not to make systematic mistakes to anticipate and mitigate the effect of a discretionary practice. The above serves as the base argument in favors of dynamically consistent plans.

These plans took the form of rules having as main objective to define the actions of the authorities in general, and particularly those of monetary management. After then, the rules became a new approach to monetary policy, with the same composition carrying an implicit target for inflation, which allows the achievement of the duty by excellence of the central institutes, which means low and stable inflation rates. Clearly possessing a target for inflation, the inflation rate through the instrument chosen (monetary aggregate or rate of interest, for example) must be the nominal anchor of the economy. This last requires, by definition, that the exchange rate regime that prevails shall be of a flexible type for not problematizing the anchoring of expectations.

As a result and considering the elements described above, what emerges today is known as "good monetary policy", the modern monetary policy, this means the *tripod* of Taylor. This trinity consists of a flexible exchange rate, a monetary policy rule and inflation-targeting approach. For this reason, the overall objective of this research is to know the theoretical foundations that comprise only two tips of the *tripod*: the rules and the whites. This is so since the exchange rate flexibility is a requirement that could be considered as a preliminary to the modern monetary policy, with the proviso that although countries claiming to be under the exchange rate regime hardly carried it out in real terms due to the set of factors present in the hypothesis raised by Guillermo Calvo and Carmen Reinhart.

In the same way, the following particular objectives will be met: *i*) establish the theoretical precepts of the scheme of inflation targeting and policy rules ii) -define the origins of inflation targeting approach, enumerating its components and which raises major criticisms of this approach, as well as some experiences, iii) establish the origin and development of the rules in order to describe the Taylor rule of 1993, identify the arguments of his main critics and those who propose them, *iv*) diagnosis of the use of inflation-targeting approach in Mexico and *v*) check if indeed the Banco de México has in its actions of some specific feature either a systematic component that describes its performance over time. These objectives will form the basis to solve both theoretical and empirical hypotheses.

It is of relevance that the evaluation of the components of the *tripod* of Taylor, since it is a system that is used in the majority of countries, both developed and emerging in development and, without a doubt, it has become the leader of issuing institutes around the world, where Mexico is no exception. In Mexico, it was necessary to gradually prepare the country (central bank) for the full adoption of an inflation-targeting approach. For this reason, it was necessary as a prerequisite of this scheme, the independence of the central bank, which was achieved through the reform of the organic law of Banco de México in 1993. In addition required to turn to the theory floating of an exchange rate regime since this was never implemented fully, due to what Calvo and Reinhart presented in 2002 as "fear of floating". This phenomenon occurs mainly in emerging economies due to the characteristics of its institutions and the lack of credibility and limited reputation of its authorities.

Given all the above elements, this research raises two theoretical hypotheses and two empirical hypotheses. The first theoretical: of an inflation-targeting approach has a number of elements that characterize it, so this can be exemplified in a more shallow way, but not so limited. This means the focus can be specified by four or five elements which, together, define it. The second theoretical: the theoretical evolution of monetary policy rules justified for its implementation as spear use in monetary policy. There are also two empirical hypotheses. The first: the Banco de México is fully guided by the precepts of inflation targeting. And the second: the Banco de México applies fully the Taylor rule, thus complying with the principle of Taylor.

CHAPTER 1

ANALYTICAL FRAMEWORK

CONTENTS

Current decisions of economic agents depend in part upon their expectations of future policy actions.

— Kydland and Prescott, 1977

Economics is a social science that seeks the explanation for human behavior as well as the structure and evolution of different variables. Human behavior tends to determine what is best given a certain context. Thus, it is evident that the performance of the variables of interest is essential to improve the well-being of humans. Thus, each and every individual forms expectations about phenomena and economic variables and therefore assumes a specific vision of how such events could happen.

The explanation and understanding of the expectations are complex and it is necessary to consider psychological foundations to "explain the functioning of the mind and reasoning" (Rubli, 2006). Mainly, in the macroeconomics area, this means that monetary theory and policy expectations are used as instruments or powerful tools for the modeling of different veins of macroeconomics.

Thus, expectations related to inflation are relevant to the modern analysis of monetary policy. Thus, when people not only believe but are convinced that inflation will rise, it is likely that actually this behavior may cause increases in prices. Therefore, if wage earners and businesses provide for increases in inflation, the former will demand wage increases and the latter will increase the prices of products and services.

Here arises a new paradigm, the hypothesis of rational expectations (HER). Under this assumption, individuals (private and public economic agents) *obtain and process* information they consider relevant, to produce a prediction or forecast of inflation. "It's like the formation of expectations was based on a known economic model, one in which the implications of the model are known" (Rubli, 2006). This is why private agents too become or are regarded as rational economic actors, because they act as if they knew the performance of the right economic model parameters.

1.1 CONDITIONAL PROBABILITY AND RATIONAL EXPECTATIONS

To fully understand the concept of rational expectations, specifically HER, and its incorporation into economic analysis, it is necessary to revise the foundations on which it is based, namely, the theory of probability. These foundations are necessary since it requires knowledge of economics and its applied field. Economic theory has always demanded the realization of expectations (expected particular values or estimated probability distributions on which is based the behavior of the market) as a condition of *the balance of the continuous state*.

Below are listed some axioms and fundamental theorems of the theory of probability, which sustain and support the validity of the rational nature of the formation of expectations of private economic actors (rationality in the sense of Muth). Having this type of agents is nothing more than connecting the economic analysis on the assumption that businesses and families operate according to the principle of low strategic interdependence of game theory and not as a power or economic position. Therefore, the basic concepts of the theory of sets and probability are the foundations of the HER, since they lay the particular situations for the acting of private agents. This means that they are the instruments necessary to the concept of conditional distribution.

Muth's theory is based on an explicit notion of rationality of expectations, but to return to it, it is necessary to have knowledge of the following axioms and theorems. In this way, any individual may have a subjective probability of distribution of a certain variable, so his/her average could exist; even if the previous values are similar, they can oscillate over a wide range, which causes the average to be not very significant. Chances are a function of the set's (probability measure) values, since this function maps real numbers to different subsets of the sample space S. Therefore, the probability axioms apply only when the sample space S is discreet.

Axiom 1. The probability of an event is a nonnegative real number; that is, $P(A) \geq 0$ for any subset A of S.

Axiom 2. $P(S) = 1$.

Axiom 3. If $A_1, A_2, A_3, \ldots$, is a finite or infinite sequence of mutually exclusive events in S, then

$$P(A_1 \cup A_2 \cup A_3 \cup \cdots) = P(A_1) + P(A_2) + P(A_3) + \cdots.$$

Theorem 1. If A is an event of a discrete sample space S, then $P(A)$ is equal to the sum of the probabilities of the individual results that make up A.

Theorem 2. If an experiment can give rise to one of N different outcomes equally and if n of these results constitute together the event, A is

$$P(A) = \frac{n}{N}.$$

This demonstrates that the classic concept of probability is consistent with the axioms of probability. The conditional probability of the event in connection with the sample space S is denoted $P(A|S)$.

Definition 1. If A and B are any two events of a sample space S and $P(A) \neq 0$, the conditional probability of B given A is

$$P(B \mid A) = \frac{P(A \cap B)}{P(A)}.$$

Theorem 3. If A and B are any two events of a space of displays S and $P(A) \neq 0$, then

$$P(A \cap B) = P(A) \times P(B \mid A).$$

Theorem 4. If A, B, and C are any three events of a space of shows S, such that $P(A) \neq 0$ and $P(A \cap B) \neq 0$, then

$$P(A \cap B \cap C) = P(A) \times P(B \mid A) \times P(C \mid A \cap B).$$

Then, according to Muth (1961), the expectations are predictions informed of future events. To have a larger picture of the expectations, it is essential to understand the concepts of probability, conditional probability, and expectation operator density. Particularly, what is intended is expanding the landscape of what exists behind the concept of rational expectations, since the set theory started the analysis of conditionality in relation to the expected value and the conditional distribution of the probability theory.

1.1.1 CONDITIONAL DISTRIBUTION

Definition 2. If $f(x,y)$ is the value of the combined probability distribution of discrete random values x and y in (x,y) and $h(y)$ is the value of the marginal distribution of y in y, the function given by

$$f(x\,|\,y) = \frac{f(x, y)}{h(y)} \quad h(y) \neq 0,$$

for x in the range of x is called a *conditional distribution* of x given $y = y$. Accordingly, if

$g(x)$ is the value of the marginal distribution of x in x, the function given by

$$w(y\,|\,x) = \frac{f(x, y)}{g(x)} \quad g(x) \neq 0,$$

for each y contained in the interval of y is called a *conditional distribution* of y given $x = x$.

Definition 3. If $f(x,y)$ is the value of the combined density of continuous random variables x and y in (x,y) and $h(y)$ is the value of the marginal density of y in y, the function given by

$$f(x\,|\,y) = \frac{f(x, y)}{h(y)} \quad h(y) \neq 0,$$

for $-\infty < x < \infty$ is called the conditional density of x given $y = y$. Correspondingly, if $g(x)$ is the value of the marginal density of x in x, the function given by

$$w(y\,|\,x) = \frac{f(x, y)}{g(x)} \quad g(x) \neq 0,$$

for $-\infty < y < \infty$ is called a *conditional density* of y given $x = x$.

Definition 4. If $f(x1, x2, ..., xn)$ is the value of the combined probability of the n distribution discrete random variables $x1, x2, ..., Xn$ in $(x1, x2, ..., xn)$ and $fi(xi)$ is the value of the marginal distribution of x, Xi for $i = 1$, $2, ..., n$, these random variables are *independent* if and only if

$$F(x1,\ x2,...,xn) = f1(x1) \times f2(x2) \times \cdots \times fn(xn),$$

for all values of $(x1, x2, ..., xn)$ contained in its range.

Definition 5. If $f(x,y)$ is the value of the combined probability distribution of discrete random variables x and y in (x, y), and $h(y)$ is the value of the marginal distribution of y in y, the function given by

$$f(x|y) = \frac{f(x,y)}{h(y)} \quad h(y) \neq 0,$$

for x in the range of x is called a *conditional distribution* of x given $y = y$. Accordingly, if $g(x)$ is the value of the marginal distribution of x in x, the function given by

$$w(y|x) = \frac{f(x,y)}{g(x)} \quad g(x) \neq 0,$$

for each y contained in the interval of y is called a *conditional distribution* of y given $x = x$.

Definition 6. If $f(x, y)$ is the value of the combined density of continuous random variables x and y in (x, y), and $h(y)$ is the value of the marginal density of y in y, the function given by

$$f(x|y) = \frac{f(x,y)}{h(y)} \quad h(y) \neq 0,$$

for $-\infty < x < \infty$ is called conditional density of x given $y = y$. In the respective form, if $g(x)$ is the value of the marginal density of x in x, the function given by

$$w(y|x) = \frac{f(x,y)}{g(x)} \quad g(x) \neq 0,$$

for $-\infty < y < \infty$ is called a *conditional density* of y given $x = x$.

The most economic applications make use of continuous random variables. If P_y is the probability that the random variable takes effectively the value of X_y, then, the vector of probabilities $P_1, \ldots, P_n$ describes the complete information about the stochastic behavior of the random variable. Thus, the expected value of a discrete random variable is

$$\text{expected value} = E(X) = \sum_{i=1}^{n} P_i \times X_i.$$

In the case of continuous random variables, the definitions are similar. Such a variable can take any value within a certain range. For continuous random variables, the expected value is defined as

$$\text{expected value} = E(X) = \int_a^b Xf(X)\,dX,$$

where a and b are the upper and lower limits respectively of the random variable. Conditioned probability or conditional density functions are widely used in the literature of rational expectations. Thus, there are two types of probability distributions. The conditional probability that depends on the occurrence or nonoccurrence of a certain event, and one that is not at the mercy of additional factors. However, economic operators will determine your chances (decisions) based on the information available at that time. Like this:

I_{t-1} : set of information available to economic operators in $t-1$.

So,

$$f(X_t \mid I_{t-1}).$$

It represents the *density of conditioned* probability of the random variable X_t, given the information available at the time $t-1$. Thus, the concept of conditional expectation is related to the conditional density and is defined as follows:

$$\text{conditional expectation}\} = E[X_t \mid I_{t-1}] = \int_a^b X_t f(X_t \mid I_{t-1})\,dX_t.$$

Thus "the conditional expectation of a random variable is the expected value of the variable, using the conditional density" (Sheffrin, 1996).

Now, we will consider the expectation conditioned as predictions of the random variables. Each of these predictions is associated with a prediction error, ε_t, which is defined as

$$\text{Forecast error}: \varepsilon_t = X_t - E[X_t \mid I_{t-1}].$$

This prediction error has two important properties:
i) The conditional expectation of the prediction error is zero[1]; thus, the conditional expectation of the prediction error is

$$E[\varepsilon_t \mid I_{t-1}] = E[X_t \mid I_{t-1}] - E[X_t \mid I_{t-1}] = 0.$$

i) The second property of the forecast errors is known as the *orthogonality* property. The forecast errors, in addition to having an expected value equal to zero, should not be correlated with any information available to economic operators.[2]

Thus, a property of conditional expectations is that the subsequent forecast errors should be inherently unpredictable and therefore not linked to any information available at the time that the prediction is formulated. The principle of *orthogonality* is expressed as follows:

$$E[\varepsilon_t \times I_{t-1} \mid I_{t-1}] = 0.$$

The prediction errors resulting from conditional expectations are not correlated with any information contained in the set of available information. The HER of Muth considered that psychological or subjective expectations of economic agents possessing the economic variables are equal to the conditional mathematical expectation of these variables.[3] Formalizing this assumption, if $_{t-1}X_t^\varepsilon$ is the psychological expectation of the variable X_t:

---

[1] At time $t-1$, conditional expectation (or prediction) is known so that its conditional expectation is the prediction itself.

[2] If this is not so, it would be possible to improve the prediction by incorporating this correlation in the forecast.

[3] This means that the subjective expectations of the people are, on average, equal to the true values of the variables.

subjective expective$\}=_{t-1} X_t^\varepsilon = E[X_t \mid I_{t-1}] = \{$conditional expective.

For this reason, in the essence of the approach of rational expectation, "exist a relationship between the beliefs of individuals and real stochastic behavior in the system" (Sheffrin, 1996). To reinforce the concept of Muth, it is necessary to make a distinction and determine the characteristics of endogenous variables and exogenous variables to the system. For the exogenous variables, predictions of the expectations of the economic agents are important; however, they do not affect the behavior of the actual values of the exogenous variables. On the other hand, expectations or predictions of the endogenous variables affect the dynamics of endogenous variables.

Therefore, the HER applies both endogenous and exogenous variables, but it is of greater interest to the implications of the latter. Expectations are rational if, given the economic model, they shed values that are equal, on average, to the expectations. Uncertainty is the only factor that causes expectations to diverge from the actual values.[4] Therefore, the HER differs from perfect forecast since its conception, it allows the existence of uncertainty in economic systems. In addition, Muth says that the expectations of the individuals should be distributed around the true expected value of the variable to be predicted.[5]

It should be noted that the HER can also be addressed from the point of view of arbitration. This leads to two points to review:

i) This hypothesis is especially applicable to financial markets in which arbitration is relatively cheap. However, I differ on this point since today, information is very expensive, especially in financial markets and, therefore, the HER is implemented with ease in this type of market. This means that the HER is applicable to financial markets because, precisely, of how costly information generates uncertainty, which becomes HER.

ii) On the other hand, the evidence that measured the beliefs or the *medium* rather than the *marginal* behavior can throw a wrong perspective of the applicability of the HER.[6] Thus, the subjective prob-

---

[4] If there is uncertainty, the expectations of the variables would agree with the actual values, in other words, would have perfect foresight.

[5] This means that the average of the individual predictions would be the expected value of the real variable, although individuals could differ in their beliefs.

[6] The HER is not synonymous with arbitration. For Sheffrin, it is possible that a market behaves in a manner consistent with this hypothesis, even when the arbitration is costly. Thus, when the arbitration is relatively inexpensive, it is better for the application of the HER.

ability distributions of economic agents match the system's objective probability distributions.[7]

1.2   REVIEWS AND CRITICISM

The HER has been subjected to much criticism and objections relating to their structural character, from critics headed by Amartya K. Sen. Authors like Swamy, Barh, and Tinsley deny the existence of objective probability distributions; on the other hand, the approach that it is prevailing, suggested by Rappoport, make the HER consistent with data used to validate the existence of objective probability distributions. Another source of controversy reviewed in this document is highlighted by Franco Modigliani. This refers to agents that are rational to form their future expectations using past information and, according to James Tobin, ensure a link between the current and future values of the economic variables. All of them are included in this section as well as the responses (criticism) associated with the same.

It is appropriate to establish that the critique of the concept of rational expectations, dictated by Amartya K. Sen, attacking the structural foundation on which it is based, i.e., it puts into question the utilitarian philosophy; therefore, it is a more general objection. This refers essentially to the philosophical understanding of the way in which man (*Homo sapiens*) became an entity that is immersed in a series of reported situations and eventualities. I mean interaction not only with their peers but with aspects of cyclical character and some others perfectly predictable that define *Homo economicus*. The latter has the ability to behave in a rational manner, which means that it responds to economic stimuli, processing information, and then acts accordingly.

Amartya Sen in his criticism of the rational of the economic agent states that the fundamental principle of Edgewoth, which assumed that all economic agents act only in their own interests is unrealistic and admits the reality that human nature has a tendency toward utilitarianism.[8] In the model of Edgeworth, which is based on selfish behavior, there is a consid-

---

[7]Muth meant that the most rational economic agents need only take into account the medium or the expected value of future variables and not worry, therefore, about high-order probability distribution. Later, Lucas (1978a) showed that it was possible to build models in which all the subjective probability distribution coincided with the real distribution of prevailing objective probability in the system.

[8]*Utilitarianism* means a conception of morality that *good* is not, but *useful*, becoming, therefore, on the *principle of utility*, a trait essential to judge the morality of our actions.

erable correspondence between the exchanges of equilibria in competitive markets and with what, in modern economic terms, is known as "the core" of the economy. "The core" of the economy is one that meets a set of conditions, i.e., "inmejorabilidad". These conditions relate to the concept of "Pareto optimal," in which no one can be better without worsening the situation of someone else.

Sen and Edgeworth say that any balance that emerges in a competitive market must meet these conditions and be in "the core." A person who begins with a bad provision could remain poor and private even after transactions. Thus, Edgeworth noted that for a good utilitarian society, competition needs to be supplemented by arbitration and the arbitration bases of the selfish are the largest total amount of utility.

For their part, and following in this tenor, Arrow and Hahn establish that an economy motivated by greed individually and controlled by a large number of agents would surely fall into a situation of chaos. For Sen, there is an additional reason for why the human behavior in economic models tends to be that of selfishness. This approach (selfishness) is also known as rational and just choosing involves internal consistency.

The election of a person is considered to be rational, if and only if, these elections can be explained entirely in terms of any relationship of preferences and be consistent with the definition of revealed preferences; this means that all elections are explained by the most preferred alternatives. The rationale of this approach, said Amartya Sen, seems to be based on the idea that the only way to understand the actual preferences of a person is by examining their current determinants or current elections and, therefore, there is no way to understand the attitude of someone using alternatives.

A consistent selector may have some degree of selfishness. This is true in the special case of the choice of the consumer's pure private property. In this case, supporters of the theory of revealed preference try to relate the preferences or the utility of the people with its own package of goods. The controversy is referred to here, because for Sen, there is no guarantee that such a package of consumption is part of a set of packages as alternatives of choice, and therefore, it is possible to expect that there is only one pack of goods on which the consumer has direct control. Sen, in this way, rejects the HER observations for the economic agent as a rational entity and it is classified as an "optimizer."

Thus, the main criticism of the HER is that it turns out to be not sufficiently general, that is, it does not include elements such as the learning and adaptive behavior. The argument of subjectivist critics Swamy, Barh, and Tinsley (1982) is the central role that the distributions of objective probability play in theory-oriented behavior. This recent theory does not like the existence of a true probability distribution or objective given the beliefs of individual agents. From the subjective point of view, the odds are essentially "betting" that an agent would be willing to perform with respect to the occurrence of a certain event.

However, when each individual bet satisfies the axioms of the theory of sets and probability, one can conclude that each individual behaves in a consistent, coherent way, and even in a rational manner. Robert E. Lucas, in response to utilitarianism and subjectivism, says that to apply economic theory in practice, it is necessary to know the agents' probability distributions. However, Lucas admits that there are situations in which the observed frequencies do not provide any guide or orientation so that agents make decisions. Under these circumstances, then, there will be no valid economic reasoning.

Another line that is controversial in this regard is suggested by Rappoport, which affirms that the primary theory of formation of expectations should be one that contrasts the hypothesis to determine if a specific mechanism of expectations ceases to be consistent with the observed data. The above is based on the scientific inference that *existing hypotheses remain until some evidence forced to reject them*. The critique of the concept of Muth refers to the role of learning, i.e., that which ensures that there is no distribution of how individuals learn certain behaviors. To this, Benjamin Friedman (1979) and Canio (1979) assert that the typical process of learning may not lead in the long term to a system like that proposed by Muth.

However, authors such as Cyert and De Groot (1974) showed that a learning process converges to the rational expectations equilibrium, so "nonconvergence" as the final result may be incorrect. For Lucas, the learning is an assumption, and therefore, the rational agent is not designed for learning.[9] In addition, Feldman (1982) and Bray and Kreps (1981) establish that if the learning process is sufficiently general, it is likely to cause a convergence toward the real, i.e., to real behavior. Therefore, these

---

[9]All private actors' learning processes are achieved through trial and error. The HER is based on the assumption that agents already carried out this process and this is how economics and competition enter different markets.

are some of the main responses to the objections of the HER with regard to the process of learning and adaptive behavior.

In practice, the HER is subjected to economic systems that are usually characterized by being immersed in uncertainty and are stochastic. Therefore, this hypothesis may be inappropriate in times of major structural changes. However, if the information is effectively free, "only the limits of Heisenberg's uncertainty principle could prevent the rational expectations hypothesis is transformed on the assumption of perfect foresight" (Sheffrin, 1996). On the other hand, if the information is scarce and has certain cost, it is important to know the specific nature of the cost function to determine the rationality in the sense of Muth. In this way, a solution to a problem of conditional maximization emerges.

Franco Modigliani also assures that the Keynesian position deteriorated when he connected the Friedman model to John Muth's HER. Modigliani attacked the HER on the basis that it is not applicable in a general way, as Senna did, but it does so from the inside of the macroeconomic models. This hypothesis states that "rational economic agents will try to form expectations of future important variables making the most efficient possible use of the information that have provided you the events of the past" (Modigliani, 1977). This contribution has had speculative applications to macroeconomics and is associated with authors such as Lucas (1972), Sargent (1976), and Sargent and Wallace (1976); this means that the hypothesis can now be named the rational expectations in macroeconomics (HERM).

The basic argument of the HERM is that the workforce in the Friedman model operates under rational expectations, implying that *i*) there can be no persistent unemployment above the natural rate, since this would mean a high serial correlation between successive errors of expectations, which is not consistent with rational expectations. In other words, the expectations of price errors are the only causes of deviations from the natural state and are random and temporary; *ii*) attempts to stabilize the economy through fiscal policy or monetary rules will be ineffective since their effect will be entirely discarded by rational expectations; and *iii*) the Government should not take *ad hoc* measures to compensate shocks since private actors are constantly covering any advance *shock*.[10]

---

[10]For this reason, government policies only may be helpful if the Government information (public) is better than the private agents. However, this is impossible by the same definition of rational expectations. In these conditions, it is more likely that the stabilization by the Government policy clashes with destabilization.

Authors such as Robert Lucas, Thomas Sargent, and Robert Barro considered standard models using expectations that are not based on full disclosure, supposing that agents possess information and their estimates of future values are regularly skewed. Furthermore, they propose to solve the problem of inconsistency in the construction of models through the acceptance of its *premise of rational*, same expectations which, given a stable structure, are confirmed to an *average* by events.

In addition, Franco Modigliani (1977) states that considering vertical long-term Phillips curve, money is neutral in the long run and keeps everything else constant; the proposal that the economy will adjust (having enough time) to a level of monetary stock held indefinitely has little practical importance, since it can be derived from a variety of models. Therefore, both micro and macroeconomics are incompatible, since Modigliani does not accept that all unemployment is "a voluntary and passed to misperceptions transient response" (Modigliani, 1977). In addition, Benjamin Friedman argues that the HERM omitted an explicit learning process and that, therefore, it should only be "interpreted as a description not in the short term but the long term balance" (Modigliani, 1977).

Therefore, its political importance is almost zero. In addition, Modigliani says, supported by Stanley Fischer, margins policy is enough to establish long-term contracts to generate wage rigidity and stabilization. Furthermore, it ensures that if the HERM deviations from the unemployment will be validated with respect to its natural rate, this would be minimal and transient. A response to this criticism is made by Sargent by adopting the hypothesis that long and lasting unemployment fluctuations are oscillations that occur at their own natural rate.

James Tobin says that the relationships between current and future values of the economic variables are essential to be considered in the economic process models: "the price of any asset today depends on its price tomorrow and after tomorrow and other future prices and, therefore, also of the determinants of these prices" (Tobin, 1980). The above applies to durable goods, for actions, for land, and also for perishable products because buyers and sellers can replace the production or consumption in a period by production or consumption in another.

To respond to the above, Arrow and Debreu suggested multiplying the number of goods to exchange by specifying the time and circumstances, the "State of nature" as they called them, in which each good would be exchanged. In addition, it was assumed that each agent has a defined vector of allocation of goods and those goods concerned utility function.[11] Given the typical assumptions applied to this list of goods, the existence of equilibrium is guaranteed and, therefore, its optimality. It only remains to arrive at a meeting date and form previously concluded contracts.

It is necessary that the States of nature are defined in such a way that the agents may not influence its occurrence or absence. Thus, it is clear that there are too many assets to maintain the *credibility* of the assumption that there are markets for all of them and that they are competitive.[12] Since we do not live in the world proposed by Arrow–Debreu, we must understand the HER as the mechanism that brings us closer and closer to face the argument of these authors and their conclusions, without the need to adopt radical assumptions. Without a doubt, economic theory requires the realization of expectations as condition of the *balance of the continued State* and the situation in which agents fail to learn from experience and act consistently based on erroneous forecasts is evidently absurd for Tobin, situations in which being outside the continuous States, the theory of rational expectations is even less precise, since "the observed results do not provide a sample of observations that conform to stationary probability distributions for the values of the variables" (Tobin, 1980).

Then, even with a stable structure, the observations are influenced by exogenous shocks that are usually difficult to detect; so, these reported results are not capable of providing a sample of repeated observations of the structure that has generated results.[13] In this way, the different potential (future) possibilities affect actual results. These future possibilities influence even if economic agents believe in the model, since this does not guarantee that these agents are in accordance with the nature and likely to different shocks.

In addition, given that rational individuals with the same information were obliged to come to the same conclusion, certain weaknesses in this theory were raised since expectations by nature are of uncertain character, so certain irrationality or differences in information is suggested. However, the majority of transactions occur because of discrepancies; this means that "*marginal* sales expectations are that determine prices in the spot and futures markets" (Tobin, 1980).

---

[11]At the beginning of the economic period, a single market of these goods determines it all, i.e., the futures market.

[12]This refers to the assumption of continuous emptying of the market, a pillar of new classical macroeconomics.

[13]The shocks are produced by policies, short-term demographics, or climatic events.

However, the marginal participants are not the same at almost any time, due to which they do not necessarily represent the average market opinion. In this type of model, the rational expectations are represented by the *statistical arithmetic* mean as the relevant behavior of an agent, given its probability distribution; so the behavior under uncertainty is very seldom an optimal strategy. "There is, in general, a linear marginal relationship between the market prices of stochastic variables and the payments for the agent that makes decisions" (Tobin, 1980).

From here, it is concluded that it should not necessarily be the value equivalent to *half* the particular figure in the variable that describes its behavior in an uncertain future. So it is impossible to predict the (future) other agents' expectations and, therefore, the expectations of other agents that will determine the values of the assets in the future. In addition, a continuous infinity of expectations is generated for certain assets (works of art, rare coins, etc.). In this regard, Keynes saw as the motive "speculation" and its persistence denoted that "marginal efficiency of capital" is both technological and psychological and, therefore, optimism is a partially independent determinant of investment and economic activity more than past and current economic conditions.

Tobin argues that it is very difficult to find a way in which expectations are formed and says that to find the most commonly used method, which is the predictive autoregression, "assuming that agents predict a variable by means of regression of their current values on their own retarded values." Tobin then comes to the conclusion that greater attention should be paid to the current data on expectations and how these are formed and less to try to define them or how they should form.

In addition, it is suitable to perform a brief analysis of the consequences of the expectations about economic policies. Thus, the structure of economic behavior that includes policy response depends on expectations with respect to the impacts of the same policy. However, if it varies regarding how to operate this policy, the estimates derived from the observations obtained during the term of a measure of economic policy will vary. So that, in circumstances of complex uncertainty, subjects responsible for decision making *usually* resort to very elementary "rules."[14]

---

[14]This means that procedures prove to be satisfactory to economic operators instead of strategies of optimization for each period and remain in use until the results get worse beyond some limit of tolerance. However, the policy change may be involved is another basic rule.

Finally, Tobin believes that the *combination* of rational expectations and market clearing concept[15] throw propositions such as "labor markets are emptied, this means is steady unemployment the full employment either that any rate of unemployment is the natural rate" (Tobin, 1980). Furthermore, for *new* monetarism, as termed by James Tobin, there is no *tradeoff* for warned macroeconomic policies since the surprises of variations in policies confuse participants in different markets, distorting their expectations, causing the emptying of the markets to happen at lower or higher rates.[16], [17]

In addition, new classical macroeconomics says that the autoregressive nature of exogenous technology shocks and the likes are the cause of "produce soft waves of observed cycles." In addition, Tobin argues that "the marginal productivities and the marginal disutility of labor are Autoregressive, stochastic processes" (Tobin, 1980). On the other hand, when there are no surprises in the policies, estimates of the price will be right and absolute variations shall be independent of absolute prices and nominal volume of expenditure.

The results of upsets are temporary, and the actual amounts seem to be positively correlated with nominal prices and policy shocks, which make them deviate from the expected. However, the observed correlation does not reveal a *tradeoff* that can be exploited systematically and repeatedly by those in charge of economic policy. This means that policy cannot achieve more than a transient distortion in actual results, changes that turn out to be insufficient. However, for Lucas, this is not true.

The main features of the "Lucas critique" are two; the first is the acceptance of the concept of rational expectations, the basic purpose of which is that it validates the other, which means the inclusion of dynamism and probability for analysis of real problems. It is clear that the use of rational expectations can be perfectly understood as an anti-Keynesian process; however, for Lucas (1987), this possibility is meaningless. Thus, the HER is assumed in shaping the new classics "as a form of micro based macroeconomics" (Contreras, 2003). The above generates forecasts and assessments that differ from traditional macroeconomics.

---

[15]When you delete the event of emptying of the market, the effects of policies on the trends of the rational expectations are zero and often stem from expectations that are not made.
[16]It is intended to establish that the results of the cooperative solutions are superior to the noncooperative solutions. This means that rules are preferred to discretion.
[17]Since the intertemporal optimization is related to both sides of the market (supply and demand), rational expectations about technology and future tastes are also relevant.

The criticism of Lucas is nothing more than an application of a principle of game theory to economics, i.e., strategic interdependence.[18] For Lucas, a change in policies that can be interpreted as a change in the macroeconomic regime will cause a change in the mode of play of agents, i.e., their spending patterns, to meet the new situation. Then, this critique argues "If the econometric models were unable to capture the new behaviour of the agents that are due to a change in policy regime, they (the models) could not correctly predict the future behavior of the economy as a whole" (Contreras, 2003).

So technically, the Lucas critique can be expressed as follows: suppose that the state of an economy in the period $t + 1$ is the function (F) itself [19] in the present period (t), where $t = 0$ is the present time of the values of the variables of politics and other exogenous variables (x) in the current period (t), the parameters that characterize the system are coordinated in a vector (θ), and the random shock[20] affecting it in the present is (ε_t), this means

$$y_{t+1} = F(y_t, x, \theta, \varepsilon_t).$$
(1.1)

Only if the function F and the vector of the parameters are known, the econometric evaluation of alternative economic policies is clear. It is important to define a policy as a specification of the present and future values of some components of x. Before this, it is necessary to derive decision rules (optimal) for agents and, if F and θ are known, it is presumed that they will remain stable and as relevant as arbitrary changes in the behavior

of the sequence x_t .[21]

Now, if the model available is reliable (F, θ) and you want to evaluate the consequences of monetary policy rules or fiscal alternatives, you could carry out simulations of the system under these policies and make a comparative evaluation. Criticism of Lucas is that all we know of dynamic economic theory indicates that the assumption of invariability of the structure is not justified when policies are changed.

The error that is incurred is the assumption that the model (F, θ) is stable under policy alternatives and changing rules, which is to assume that

---

[18]Participants of any game will modify its behavior if the rules of the game change, in order to improve their results.
[19]It is represented by a vector of variables [y].
[20]Random shocks are independent and identically distributed.
[21]Decision rules are expressed as functions of supply and demand.

the expectations of agents with respect to the possible behavior of shocks in the system are invariant. The reaction of agents is to softly or suddenly adapt the decision rules as they are willing to predict what changed over time. In addition "recognizes and approves the denial of Thomas Cooley Edward Prescott of refusing to make the vector θ fixed and characterized it as a random variable" (Contreras, 2003) and whose behavior is as follows:

$$\theta_{t+1} = \theta_t + \eta_{t+1},$$

$$(1.2)$$

where η_t is a sequence of independent and identically distributed random variables. The Cooley–Prescott approach is called adaptive regression because it mimics the exponential smoothing of observations, where they receive one lower weighting observation of the more distant past. If policies are considered stochastically distributed functions of the state of the system, where there is a vector of fixed parameters λ and one of η disturbances, and a parameter θ, behavior is

$$x_t = G(y_t, \lambda, \eta_t),$$

$$(1.3)$$

$$y_{t+1} = F(y_t, x_t, \theta(\lambda), \varepsilon_t).$$

$$(1.4)$$

Then the problem is to estimate the function $\theta(\lambda)$, and policy is defined here as a change in the parameters λ or the function that generates the values of the variables of politics. Thus, a change in policy (at λ) affects the performance of the system in two ways: i) to alter the behavior of the time series of x_t and ii) to cause modification of the parameters of the $\theta(\lambda)$ behavior of the rest of the system. Lucas concurs with Muth in the sense that the conditional forecast of predictive capabilities for data agents does not determine immediate and instantaneous real structure of the policies in which they are immersed.[22]

Furthermore, Lucas states that responses of agents are predictable, if and only if, others share certain vision about the nature of shocks to predict. The above leads us to "solution of Lucas" which opts in favor of the above discretionary policies rules. Thus, Lucas completes a final reflection

---

[22]Therefore, if policy changes are widely understood by agents such as changes in the rules, there is no more likelihood that structural changes are correctly predicted with past estimates of $\theta(\lambda)$.

on the matter in the form of conclusion, which is expressed in the following syllogism.[23]

"That *i*) the structure of an econometric model consists of optimal decision rules for agents and *ii*) optimal decision rules vary systematically,
you change the structure of the series that are relevant to decision making, *i* and *ii* follow c) any change in the policy to systematically alter the
structure of the econometric models" (Contreras, 2003). That is that if
policymakers making economic policies want to improve their ability to
forecast with respect to the answers of the agents, they need to implement
clearer rules and explain any changes in these widely.

Potential policies affect the allocation of resources and individual welfare, so that in practice, economic policy discussions are relevant. In this
regard, only the reason why remains to be added: Robert Lucas put forth
his criticism: such motivation is expressed in that agents, technology preferences, and the rules of the game are variant components over time and
depend on the policy changes. In this way, "true social science modeling is
not more than an attempt to *understand* human behavior and incorporating
in all its complexity, its present and future options" (Contreras, 2003), i.e.,
the range of reactions to the environment variable.

For this reason, given the different decisions of private agents in situations of uncertainty and, in the context of better monetary policy, it is necessary to take into consideration the relevance of credibility and reputation
and the preference for cooperative solutions for a central bank. In this way,
authors and Nobel Prize winners, Kydland and Prescott developed and
sustained, under these conditions, the concept of dynamic inconsistency.
This contribution is critical when it comes to monetary policy in different
institutes of the planet since it emanates the possibility to optimize certain
monetary policy. Thus, we will focus the next section of this chapter to
explain this concept more accurately.

1.3   DYNAMIC INCONSISTENCY AND TAYLOR TRIPOD

The argument that lies around the use of rules versus discretion has as
major defenders of the rules Friedman, Edward Prescott, and Finn E. Kydland. The fundamental characteristic of the first is that since those who
implement policies do not know the effect and timing of monetary poli-

---

[23]Syllogism is a deductive reasoning consisting of two propositions as premises and a conclusion, the
latest being necessarily deductive inference from the other two.

cies, the recommended action is the implementation of these policies by using rules. Even knowing the effects and temporality, the use of rules is also recommended due to the dynamic inconsistency problem.

The Nobel Prize laureates Finn E. Kydland and Edward Prescott, in 2004, analyzed the way in which economic agents make decisions considering the behavior of future variables with a paper regarding the temporary inconsistency in monetary policy. They define a consistent policy selected as the best option in each period, given the current economic situation.[24] The above presents an unintended consequence; this means a suboptimal result since the authorities do not consider the future decisions of agents.

Figure 1.1 represents some of Phillips and indifference curves (Kydland and Prescott, 1977). Equilibrium is consistent when the indifference curve is tangential to a Phillips curve at a point of the vertical axis, as in point C. Only then there are rational expectations and the selected policy is best, given the current situation. Indifference curves imply that "socially preferred inflation rate is zero" (Kydland and Prescott, 1977), which is consistent with the public preferences.[25] If this was so, x_t should be interpreted as a deviation from the optimal rate. This suggests that the result of the selection was a consistent policy, which was clearly not optimal.

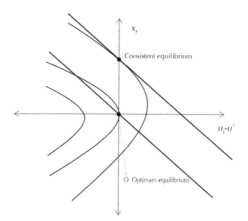

FIGURE 1.1   Consistent and Optimal Equilibrium.
(From Kydland, F., and Prescott, E., J. Polit. Econ., 85, 3, 1977. With permission.)

---

[24]A policy is inconsistent when it ceases to be the best choice for the next period.
[25]Note that here, inflation is a tax and, therefore, a more informed public prefers any positive or negative inflation rate.

In this way, if policymakers were forced to maintain price stability and were able to start discretionary policies, the resulting equilibrium could be unemployment not higher to that obtained by the policy. Thus, according to Kydland and Prescott, the optimal balance O, which was located on a curve of indifference, was higher than that of the consistent equilibrium point C. These authors describe that Taylor (1995) found that the optimal monetary policy is random in a world of rational expectations, a result similar to that Kydland and Prescott arrived at in this problem by introducing uncertainty in the social objective function.[26]

Even when there are fixed or perfect objective social functions and those responsible for the implementation of monetary policy have knowledge regarding the timing and magnitude of the effects of their actions, discretionary policy,[27] not function, maximizes social objective. This, according to Kydland and Prescott, is because economic planning is not a game against nature, but a game against rational economic agents. So, these authors defend the thesis that "there is no applicable control theory to economic planning" (Kydland and Prescott, 1977). The theory of optimal control is a device useful for situations in which results and movements of the state of the system depend only on the current and past policy decisions. However, the Kydland–Prescott approach argues that this is unlikely in the case of dynamic economic systems and holds that the current or present decisions of economic agents are in function, partly, future expectations of policy actions.[28]

There are factors that can modify the social objective function. For example, a change in the administration has immediate effects on the expectations of agents, which modify their current decisions. The above does not imply that private economic operators are able to make perfect forecasts of future policies. In summary, Kydland and Prescott claim that agents have "some" knowledge of how the decisions of those responsible for implementation of policies will be changed as a result of changes in economic conditions.

However, Lucas (1976) says that given that optimal decision rules vary systematically, any change in policy will alter the structure of these rules. Thus, the essential objective of this pair of economists is the concept of

---

[26]Then, the optimal policy is consistent and, therefore, it is not recommended for the central banker to continue with the original policy rules.

[27]Kydland and Prescott define a discretionary policy such as that selected by policymakers given the current situation. This does not necessarily imply that the social function is the maximized objective.

[28]Only if these expectations are invariant in time, the selected policy plan might be appropriate.

"policy"; they try to explain the problem "of two periods," demonstrating that a consistent policy is suboptimal. In addition, the theory of optimal control for the problem of management of aggregate demand turns out to be also irrelevant when the rational expectations modeling technique is incorporated. Thus, in "balance, optimizers agents follow rules that specify current decisions as a function of the present state" (Kydland and Prescott, 1977).[29]

The Kydland–Prescott approach is also based on the criticism of Lucas and the effects that changes in economic policies have on private agents. Kydland and Prescott argue that in a dynamic economic system, the agents form their expectations taking into account possible changes in policy, which affects their current decisions. The omission of expectations gives rise to the authorities carrying out discretionary management. Then, policies are inconsistent because they are suboptimal solutions, since they are only valid for a period (the current) and not for the long term.

Dynamic inconsistency arises since it is convenient for the authorities (optimal) to exploit the surprise factor; however, the existence of rational individuals prevents authorities from exploiting the unexpected element on a permanent basis. Authorities do realize that they cannot deceive the public constantly and carry out a reassessment of their objectives by applying new policy changes. This allows central bankers to recover surprise policy effects.

It could be when you reach this point we can say that an institution with a low degree of credibility confronts the problem of dynamic inconsistency because of the sum set of discretionary policies and its lack of commitment to the public. The fixing of the exchange rate has proven to be a mechanism against dynamic inconsistency when monetary authorities in a given country do not enjoy sufficient credibility and reputation; this means that the country imports credibility of another country through the pegs.

Recently, in practice, there has been a trend toward the reduction and elimination of discretionary actions by establishing policy rules that set goals or objectives. The best example of this is the policy that gives priority to the stability of prices in the medium and long terms. If a policy of this kind is to be efficient, the authorities of the central institute should strengthen their commitment to the public to increase the confidence re-

---

[29]Within the classification of policy feedback rules, we found that the optimal rule depends on the conditions or initial endowments. For this reason, Kydland and Prescott said that is not optimal to continue with the initial policy in subsequent periods. The previous concept is also known as the optimal policy inconsistency.

garding the continuity of economic policy in general, in particular the monetary policy.

An additional component that has become determinant in terms of objectives is the strategy of monetary policy known as inflation-targeting approach (IT). It has also helped improve communication between private plans of the central banker, policy, and agents. Thus, the constant reiteration of the commitment of the authorities with families and businesses contributes to minimizing the problem of temporary inconsistency. Inflation targeting is based on rules as a stabilizing component. This approach works by the announcement of the central bank of a target for inflation.

This announcement must not necessarily be an explicit number; this implies that to achieve the target of inflation posed as monetary policy, it is necessary to act through rules, which, in turn, operate through some discretion. Pragmatically, inflation targeting is part of a more complex concept in which the interest rate is set as the nominal anchor of the economy; in addition to that, a prerequisite for the approach, the exchange rate regime should be flexible. This is essential, because otherwise, with the exchange rate fixed, the economy would be subject to two nominal anchors, which – far from providing stability – insert (together) uncertainty among private agents.

Thus, the determination of modern monetary policy lies on a basis including concepts such as rational expectations, the commitment of the authorities to achieve the long-term goals (targets), and rules of monetary policy, particularly the rule of Taylor, reference to which will be made in Chapter 3 of this research. Thus, for the development and management of a good monetary policy aimed at emerging economies, Taylor (2000c) proposed a Trinity composed of IT, a monetary policy rule, and a flexible exchange rate.

For this reason, having inflation targeting is essential to implement a good monetary policy in those cases where countries decide to adopt a flexible exchange rate regime. This is how the inflation target assumes the role of nominal anchor of domestic prices rather than the type of flexible exchange or a dollarization. However, empirical evidence has fully demonstrated that the combination of flexible exchange rate, inflation targeting, and policy rules not only have operated successfully in emerging countries but have also been effective in developed countries.

If the inflation rate is the target, then the value at which this target should be around is the current rate of inflation, according to Taylor (2000c). A good monetary policy therefore implies that the standard deviations should be minimal and credible. It is important to emphasize that having a target of inflation does not mean that the issuing institute should necessarily announce an explicit numeric value. The target may be indirect or implicit. Taylor believes that the specific target of inflation is to set goals, but condition some particular ratings as price stability.

However, for a central bank, possessing a target for the inflation rate is not enough. There are different policies (including the use of different instruments) that allow achieving a long-term inflation target.[30] Therefore, the choice of an inflation target still leaves open most of the fundamental issues of monetary policy decisions. It is at this point that the rules of monetary policy emerge as the method by which monetary policy will lead to the achievement of the inflation target described above.

Then, "the policy rules provide details about the way in which will be reaching the target" (Taylor, 2000c). In the absence of a good policy rule, you will never get to reach the raised target or you'll punctually get target but after altering the average behavior of other relevant variables, which will force the central banker to abandon it due to the presence of an expensive event in social terms and reputation and credibility of the issuing institute, such as high inflation and disinflation.

So, Taylor says that to carry out a good monetary policy given the local and international context of different economies; whether it is small or large, it is necessary to adopt a flexible exchange rate regime, enabling the central banker to set nominal anchors to the interior of the country and thus, not depend on external exchange rate fluctuations. Therefore, "for a country that has not chosen, temporarily, to fix their exchange rate through a currency board, or some kind of dollarization, the only alternative that can work well in the long run for monetary policy is one that is based on the tripod: flexible exchange rate, inflation-targeting approach and monetary policy rule." (Taylor, 2001).

The mentioned triad is named the Taylor tripod, whose main objective is to overcome the problem posed by Kydland and Prescott's temporary inconsistency, i.e., the inflationary bias. Monetary inflation targeting regimes need a procedure to achieve such target, and policy rules are one of the main mechanisms to achieve this. Therefore, all of monetary regimes based on IT require for their operation and good performance, policy rules.

---

[30]Some policies consider inflation fluctuations around others much larger than target. Other policies will cause greater fluctuations for other nominal and real variables of interest to central bankers, such as exchange rate and the actual product.

Then, a good monetary policy rule is one in which fluctuations in inflation observed with respect to their target are the children.

However, it is possible to establish other types of targets for other variables provided that said target is consistent with the long-term inflation target. For example, the target for the product should be the natural rate of production; for the exchange rate, the appreciation or depreciation for target shall be the difference between the rate of domestic inflation and the inflation rate average of other countries. Once the different targets are consistent in the long run, then a *tradeoff* between variabilities occurs, i.e., between trying to keep small fluctuations around the target of inflation and fluctuations around other targets.

It is important to highlight that policy rule instructs the central banker on how to choose a point in the *tradeoff*. The earlier exchange replaces the exchange described in the traditional Phillips curve. Both J. Taylor and Donald Brash[31] establish that the IT "is not the remedy for everything". This means that they do not constitute a guarantee against errors of monetary policy. In short, Taylor explains that for the successful implementation of the targets of inflation, a procedure policy (a policy rule) is necessary to achieve the designated target.[32] These elements will be studied separately in the following two chapters.

Chapter 2 is dedicated to studying the IT, essentially elaborating on obstacles and facilities that have faced both developed and emerging countries. In addition, this chapter reviews the major objections to the IT's personalities' experience and knowledge to validate them. Chapter 3 has the aim of studying the policy rules with special emphasis on the "Taylor rule." They will be raised such that they arise from the need to limit the actions and the power of the State and, in this way, establish systematic behavior within the different Governments. Finally, criticisms that have more harmed the arguments of its most ardent defenders are set out.

---

[31]The Reserve Bank Governor in New Zealand, a pioneer in the implementation of the IT.

[32]The analogy used by Taylor to express the relationship between inflation targeting and the policy rules is as follows: inflation targeting is the destination for a boat. And the policy rule is the way, processes, and procedures necessary to reach the destination, i.e., the boat.

KEYWORDS

- **Economic variables**
- **Human behavior**
- **Rational expectations**
- **Conditional distribution**
- **Utilitarianism**
- **Conditional density**

CHAPTER 2

INFLATION-TARGETING APPROACH

CONTENTS

Inflation targeting is very much a "look at everything" strategy, albeit one with a focused goal.

—Bernanke, Laubach, Mishkin, and Posen, 2001

Inflation-targeting approach (IT) is a monetary policy regime designed for central banks to manage to get low and stable rates of inflation. The origin of the targets of inflation in the 1990s was proposed without too many academic elements or for research. Therefore, the practices of the different central banks have strengthened the focus gradually such that we reach certain consensus for international acceptance. It is possible to identify some items that are common in the design and implementation of this regime.

These aspects are divided into institutional and operational. The first refers to the initial conditions under which a central bank must be based to launch an inflationary program based on targets. Inflation targeting requires that the institutional commitment that one orient the issuing institution to achieve price stability is constantly validated. In addition, it is necessary that the central bank enjoys – and is in constant search for – a high level of credibility so that the expectations of the agents are anchored, and thus converged inflation target is established.

IT refers basically to three components: *i*) the public announcement of the inflation target, *ii*) the efficient identification of inflationary pressures, and *iii*) the improvement of the communication mechanisms that ensure transparency in information plans and decisions of the central bank. The above elements allow one to spur the central bank to achieve the target for inflation with greater ease and professionalism since it directly influences the expectations of private economic agents. The components listed earlier will be reviewed extensively throughout this chapter.

2.1   ORIGINS AND EVOLUTION

The construction of the IT was conceived in practice by the theoretical documents of the case of collaborations between central bankers, where each of them shared their first experiences on the results of the application of this approach in their own country, i.e., empirically derived from a fundamental process. The central bank of New Zealand (Reserve Bank of New Zealand) was the first institution to implement this approach in

1990. Subsequently, this scheme was adopted by countries like Canada in 1991, the UK in 1992, and Australia and Sweden a year later. The Czech Republic, as a developing country, was the first to establish the operational framework and Chile was the first Latin American economy to do so.[1]

Among the main actions taken is the Decree of stability in the general level of prices as the sole purpose, and for better operation of that provision, it was to be done jointly by the Governor of the central bank and the Finance Minister. This provision allowed some exceptions, which permitted to temporarily leave the band set at the IT. This marked the beginning of this monetary regime and as can be seen, from its very conception, it allows deviations from its goal.

The circumstances in which the country (New Zealand) was before the official announcement of the IT were high inflation and a weak output in terms of growth. So the Organization outlined and emphasized credibility programs for monetary authorities, promoting commitment and transparency in their actions. Along these lines, so that monetary policy would be credible, it was necessary to show that it was not an ad only; so monetary expansion was reduced. Agreements of "target" of inflation included the possibility of deviations for the achievement of the goal to short-term events (natural disasters, changes) in the form of government, higher taxes, etc. The result was the rapid decrease of the inflation rate even below the stipulated level.

IT is a policy regime that has been lately adopted by many developed countries such as Canada, the UK, New Zealand, Sweden, Australia, and Spain and by the European Central Bank. Among the economies of emerging countries are Brazil, Chile, and Mexico. Inflation targeting is a mechanism that reduces the desire for policy discretion by the authorities' and reduces the costs of the process of deflation, while it increases the credibility of the monetary authorities. However, the expected inflation rate and, therefore, inflation expectations will be reduced, provided the central bank demonstrates that it is able to obtain low inflation rates.

Inflation targeting should be understood as "a policy framework that increases the credibility of the monetary authorities through transparency and the ability to maintain some level of consistency in situations in which the policy discretion arises" (Bernanke and Mishkin, 1997). Monetary au-

---

[1]There is a debate that this has not yet been defined in the sense that Chile began to implement the inflation targeting in unison with New Zealand. For its part, Mexico officially adopted the scheme in 2001.

thorities make use of complementary measurements of inflation, such as underlying inflation, to isolate those phenomena that transiently affect inflation and identify the trend of medium-term growth of prices. The calculation of underlying inflation serves to minimize variations in the National Index of Consumer Prices (Indice Nacional de Precios al Consumidor), stabilize, and eliminate – in a specific way – strong fluctuations in the level of prices.

However, the successful application of the system of inflation targeting requires consideration of all the characteristics of the country, as well as the inherent consequences of such application to the stabilization of prices, and is relatively simple. The substantial contribution of inflation targeting is that the authorities settle for shorter time periods (a year), thus, the authorities create certainty and trust among agents. It is important to stress that, as Bernanke and Mishkin propose, the stability of prices does not mean in practice that inflation equals zero.

The literature lays special emphasis on establishing that it is really difficult to forecast inflation, particularly for very short and very long periods. This lack of predictability can impose two problems in the design of the strategy of target inflation. The first is strictly operational: given that the effects of monetary policy are reflected with significant lags, exact predictability of inflation targeting is very difficult. The second relates to the credibility of the central bank: if inflation is difficult to predict and difficult to control, so is it difficult to determine whether the efforts of the central bank are sufficient for the achievement of the inflation target.

The actions of monetary policy carried out by a central bank affect the economy, in particular, the level of prices, with some lag. Therefore, to achieve inflation targeting, the Monetary Authority must make its *decisions* based on a thorough evaluation of the economic situation and prospects on the inflationary conditions facing the country. The characteristics and structural elements of IT in different countries will be revised in this chapter.

2.2 COMPONENTS AND EXPERIENCES

There are four fundamental components offered by Bernanke and Mishkin (1997).

i) Inflation targeting performs "an official announcement of a medium-term target for the inflation rate up to one or more horizons, usually from one to three years" (Bernanke and Woodford, 2005).

ii) They make explicit that a low and stable (nominal target) rate of inflation is the main objective of monetary policy.

iii) This approach includes in its structure the increase of communication with the public on plans and objectives of the monetary authorities.

iv) Finally, IT provides a very active transparency policy, making explicit the intentions of the central bank to improve the planning of the private sector, publicly discussing the orientation of monetary policy.

However, as shown in the revised literature, complementary elements of fundamental components arise, as follows.

v) This scheme assumes monetary neutrality, i.e., that the monetary variables do not affect the actual variables in the long run; however, in the short term, changes in monetary variables can have significant effects on real variables. But, this does not imply that the central bank assumes inflation as an essentially monetary phenomenon.

Inflation targeting is a regime of monetary policy that could well be called a "hybrid" and, at the same time, a multipurpose mechanism. The above based on such an approach, in its structure, both contains classic elements of inflation and, at the same time, avoids Keynesian arguments. There is no theory of inflation that dominates; rather the IT has an understanding of inflation both by demand (classical theory) and costs or offer (theory of neo-Keynesian inflation). Those who use inflation targeting do not make explicit that it must be accompanied by a policy rule; however, they argue that its implementation is essential to following a systematic component without specifying that this should be a rule.

On the other hand, the authors identify the way central bank attacks supply shocks as one of the main disadvantages of inflation targeting. Here, it is derived that "shocks" not anticipated in the price level could be interpreted as "past" and, therefore, never be compensated. The consequence of this is that the forecast of the level of prices over long horizons could have large variances, which would prevent the planning of the private sector (Bernanke and Mishkin, 1997). Thus, there are four components of the IT.

vi) IT excludes from its structure (of the index on which it is based) the effects of first round of shocks , such as the prices of energy, food, and value-added taxes. This means that it is recommended based on the index of underlying inflation. However, the Banco de México used the general rate of inflation as the basis of the inflation targeting.

vii) Point number (i) states that that official announcement can be set up in ranges or by a specific number. However, the use of ranges in this approach reflects uncertainty and imposes a degree of uncertainty around private agents when making decisions. Despite this drawback, these ranges give flexibility for the short-term policymaker.

viii) Since inflation targeting allows monetary authorities to enjoy discretion (based on the use of ranges specified in the previous point), the short- and medium-term targets can be adjusted to accommodate supply shocks or other exogenous changes that are beyond the control of the central bank.

So, the discretion referred to earlier is communicated to the public as a mechanism that pursues the announced inflation target-oriented path.

ix) Note the previous point that this approach assumes the possibility of deviations from the target of inflation in order to minimize the real cost, i.e., the performance of the product. Thus, authorities can "announce" the modification of the medium-term inflation target without affecting the long-term target.

x) The approach "un-emphasizes" intermediate targets as the exchange rate and the amount of money. In the same way, the IT view also loses on additional objectives that could follow the monetary policy, such as: the promotion of employment and the gross domestic product. This does not mean that the regime that operates is single-purpose inflation targeting, but that it can be implemented under a hierarchical regime.

xi) Finally, Bernanke and Mishkin argue that moderate inflation is not necessarily bad and propose that 4% is a level of inflation that can be sustainable, i.e., it can register acceptable growth rates of the gross domestic product without compromising the primary objective of the approach (the inflation) risk.[2]

Once the different components of this scheme are established, some of them may seem redundant; therefore, it is possible to combine some of them to make their characterization more compact.

---

[2]All the features addressed with respect to the inflation-targeting approach were consulted from the works of Bernanke and Mishkin (1997), Bernanke, Laubach, Mishkin, and Posen (2001), and Bernanke and Woodford (2005).

Then, it is evident that point (i) makes it obvious that inflation is the primary objective of monetary policy, from which is derived point (ii). It can be added to the first, and in addition, it is possible that point (vii) complements it. Given the above, it is necessary to argue that there is evidence that this approach "increases the professionalism in decision-making and increases the political acceptance" (Bernanke and Woodford, 2005) because it effectively improves decision making. I also think points (iii) and (iv), refer to very similar elements, which could be addressed as a set of policies to improve communication with the public through actions of transparency aimed at strengthening the credibility and reputation of the central bank.

Also, it would be helpful to group subparagraphs (viii) and (ix), since inflation targeting can be set in ranges and hence the possibility of deviations from the target to minimize actual costs is latent. In this way, discretion should be established as a mechanism that pursues the announced inflation target-oriented path. Finally, this section asserts that inflation targeting is not a rule because *i*) it does not provide an operational mechanism to the central bank and *ii*) it possessed a considerable degree of discretion.[3] The above must be accompanied by a system check and the implications of discretionary long-term actions evaluated in the short and medium terms; thus, inflation targeting helps to discipline the monetary policy.[4]

In this manner, one can individually identify five fundamental components that characterize the IT, completely condensed already in points (v) and (vi). Similarly, it is appropriate to add some more important features to this approach:

xii) Establish that when the target limits are exceeded or the target is not reached, the central bank is in need of "greenwash" of the situation too. This not only reduces the variance in the prognosis of long-term prices but also injects greater volatility to the monetary policy in the short term. This reflects the necessity of how the central bank intends to defend its reputation and prestige.

---

[3]Bernanke and Mishkin considered inflation targeting as a structure for the monetary policy in which limited discretion may apply. This structure provides improvements in communication between authorities and the public and increases the discipline of monetary policy.

[4]In practice, the need for discipline differs from country to country since it depends on politicians, institutional arrangements, and personalities. A country needs discipline when it comes to reducing the rate of unemployment below its natural level, fooling the public to increase inflation and thus the product. However, this cannot be taken constantly since it would mean misleading workers and firms consistently and sequentially.

Another way to do this is through an "escape clause" that allows central banks and Governments to suspend or modify the schema of inflation targeting under very adverse economic situations.

xiii) This approach does not imply a unique mandate for the monetary policy regime; so in addition to stabilizing inflation, it seeks to stabilize other real and nominal variables (gross domestic product and the exchange rate) and thereby achieve financial stability.

Therefore, the designations of monetary policy in developed and emerging economies are different since the monetary regime of inflation targeting "allows much discretion to policymakers in a very weak institutional environment which brings as a consequence poor macroeconomic results" (Mishkin, 2004).

The implementation of the IT is necessary, as mentioned above, as a monetary policy framework, taking into account the particular characteristics of each country, idiosyncratic risks associated with it, and at the same time proper evaluation of the economic situation. For precisely this reason, there are fundamental differences among different countries. Fundamental differences between developed and developing countries are considerable and characterizing the conditions of the latter is evidence that it is actually more complicated to obtain satisfactory results under an inflation-targeting regime in such countries.

i)   Weaknesses in fiscal institutions;
ii) Inefficient financial institutions in relation to the recruitment of national savings and fragile prudential regulation and supervision;
iii) Low credibility of their monetary institutions;
iv) Potential replacement of the currency and any other currency (dollarization dependence);
v)   Vulnerability to sudden capital inflows.

Developed countries are immune with their fiscal, financial, and monetary institutions, while developing countries are highly vulnerable to high levels of inflation rate and exchange rate crises. For Mishkin (2004), a necessary condition for the control of inflation is fiscal stability also: due to the perceived needs,[5] the tax authorities can press and persuade monetary authorities on the benefits of hiring debt, producing a rapid growth of the circulating currency and, therefore, a high inflation rate.

So, if unbalanced fiscal balances are large enough, eventually the monetary policy becomes subordinate to fiscal considerations and validates the

---

[5]Mishkin refers to these needs as possible listed authorities' "irresponsible" actions.

process called *fiscal domination* (Mishkin, 2004). Thus, inflation targeting may be abandoned or seriously modified. In the same way, a solid financial system is also a necessary condition for the success of the analyzed monetary regime. A weak banking system is particularly dangerous, since in these conditions, you cannot grow interest rates to maintain the target of inflation because these revised interest rates can lead to the collapse of the financial system. In addition, this can lead to exchange rate disorder and, subsequently, a financial crisis that, in turn, limits the control of prices.

Now, when the markets recognize the weakness of the banking system, there will be an imminent capital outflow from the country, which will result in strong depreciation or devaluation (as the case may be) of the local currency, which at the same time leads to upward pressure on the inflation rate. In addition, as a result of the devaluation of the currency, which probably will be accompanied by monetary expansion, the debt of the national companies that are denominated in a foreign currency rises, whereas assets denominated in national currency grow at a much slower rate and, finally, register a decrease in equity of the companies.[6]

This deterioration of the balance sheets of firms reduces access to credit markets, leading to a decline in investment and, hence, economic activity and finally to the absolute collapse of the banking system. Later comes the "bank bailout," which gives rise to an enormous increase in the Government's liabilities that must be paid in the future, acting to the detriment of the IT. Due to the above considerations, it is necessary to determine from the outset whether inflation targeting will be an effective instrument of monetary policy to keep inflation under control.

Avoiding financial instability requires several types of institutional reforms. First, prudential regulation of the banking and financial systems must be strengthened to prevent these types of crisis. Secondly, the security provided by the local government network may need to be limited in order to reduce the likelihood that banks engage in high-risk activities. Third, the government should seek to limit exchange rate imbalances in order to avoid devaluation or depreciation of the currency and this deterioration of the financial statements of domestic enterprises.[7]

---

[6]This balance-sheet deterioration causes increased *adverse selection* and moral hazard in credit markets.

[7]A devaluation of the currency is adopted under the fixed exchange rate regime, while a depreciation comes in the flexible exchange rate regime.

The effects (benefits) of inflationary impact due to activities carried out by monetary authorities "are lower in emerging and developing countries due to different factors" (Barro and Gordon, 1983):
i)   Wariness of agents on decisions of the monetary authority (little credibility);
ii) The fear that possible inflation far expands economic activity, generating national and international uncertainty and reductions in domestic consumption;
iii) It is difficult to accept that the expansion of economic activity is accompanied by a reduction in the supported unemployment rate,
iv) The initial cost of a discretionary policy is the increase in expectations of future inflation; and
v)   Underdeveloped financial system.

Obviously the first, second, and third points relate essentially to the fact that reputation and credibility enjoyed by the monetary authorities in emerging and developing countries is minimal or insignificant since these countries are still in the process of stabilization of their economic fundamentals, which causes constant and undefined variations of given macroeconomic aggregates.

It is important to highlight the initial circumstances under which inflation targeting is implemented in different countries, such as their level of development, their idiosyncrasies, the degree of credibility of their institutions, etc. As well as, during the period from 1985 to 1989, before the adoption of the IT, countries such as Australia, Canada, Chile, Finland, Israel, New Zealand, Spain, Sweden, and the UK underwent an average of 15% inflation and annual growth of 7.5% after 1993 until 1997; once the scheme was adopted, the same countries experienced average inflation of 3.3% with an average rate of growth of 6.9%.

Similarly, countries such as Canada, Iceland, Norway, the UK, and Turkey adopted specific targets; Sweden, Brazil, Chile, Hungary, Mexico, Peru, Philippines, Poland, and the Czech Republic did so through a timely target range of variability, while Australia, New Zealand, Switzerland, Colombia, Israel, South Africa, and Thailand did so through the application of ranges of tolerance (Ortiz, 2012). It is necessary to note that Canada, Norway, Iceland, and the UK have a punctual target and a range that is used only as a reference to provide explanations to the public when inflation deviates from target.

New Zealand has a small open economy and had announced a series of innovative reforms. These reforms helped to restrict the variations in inflation, specifically a significant fiscal consolidation, changes to the labor market, and greater reductions of trade barriers. In addition, in the monetary field, policy was oriented to a context of accountability. The Governor of the central bank would have to define explicit policy objectives, and his/her performance would be judged. A key aspect here is to note that since New Zealand is an emerging economy, these reforms did not result in problems or influence other countries.

In 1991, Canada adopted the IT. The independence of the central bank as a prerequisite was necessary for its implementation, and then 3% target was established and currently uses a range of 1–3%.[8] The Bank of Canada is (as most of the banks) governed under a hierarchical command and the actions taken by the monetary authorities to give credibility to the announced target were restricted fiscal policy and launch of a campaign of communication with the public. The result was the stability and reduction of prices, and the inflation rate remained within the established bands. However, since the mandate in this country is hierarchical, completeness could not be achieved due to the fact that the unemployment rate rose to 10%.

On the other hand, the UK adopted inflation targeting since 1992. King, Governor of the Bank of England for a long time, shared his experience and said that although the adoption of the IT in the UK did not form an essential part of the improvement of macroeconomic performance, this scheme allowed the making of right decisions easier. In addition, he noted that this approach increased the professionalism in the decision making, which in turn increased political acceptance. Finally, he argues that this approach should be seen as "a way of thinking politics" or as "a way of implementing the optimal policy" (King, 2005; Bernanke and Woodford, 2005).

2.3 MAIN CRITICISMS

Since its conception, inflation targeting has been an outline of monetary policy and has generated many questions about its functioning, structure, and results. A series of criticisms that attack the above-mentioned elements

---

[8]In 1991, when the Central Bank of Canada met with its counterparts from the G-10, the announcement that that country would take the IT as the basic axis of its monetary policy was not well received. The members of this group of countries conceived not why a country with a prudent central bank would risk their reputation by adopting an explicit mandate.

emerge from there. Some are listed below. Much of the observations on the IT are essentially related to its discretionary nature and that, therefore, it can be understood as a source of uncertainty.

i) The use of ranges in this approach reflects uncertainty and imposes a degree of uncertainty about the private agents when making decisions. Despite this, these ranges gives flexibility to short-term policymakers.

ii) When the target limits are exceeded or not reached, the central bank has the need to "manufacture" the situation too. This reduces the variance of the prognosis of long-term prices but injects greater volatility to monetary policy in the short term. This necessity reflects on how the central bank intends to defend its reputation and prestige.

iii) Another way to do this is through an "escape clause" that allows central banks and governments to suspend or modify the schema of inflation targeting under very adverse economic situations.

iv) In emerging markets, it is difficult to implement inflation targeting (Calvo and Mishkin, 2003) because of weak financial institutions, limited prudential regulation and supervision of the Government, low credibility of the monetary institution, and vulnerability to sudden "braking" of capital flows.

v) Monetary, financial, and fiscal weakness makes markets extremely vulnerable to high inflation and exchange rate crises in emerging economies.

One of the most representative critiques about the operability of international inflation targeting is that performed by the professor of economics at Leuven University and member of the *Group* of *Economic Policy Analysis* of Belgium, De Grauwe. The fundamental argument of the Member of the Belgian Parliament is that there are many more central banks to be brought under inflation targeting; this means that not all issuing institutions around the world operate under this scheme. In addition, De Grauwe said that the subprime crisis has made it clear that central banks cannot take responsibility for the prevention of bubbles and the supervision of all institutions that are in the business of creating credit and liquidity.

De Grauwe affirms that the central banks are unable to identify and predict the formation of bubbles in the different markets. He acknowledges, however, that when a central bank somehow manages to detect a particular market bubble, the effects of the crisis are limited as soon as the central bank returns the rate of inflation to normal levels. Continuing with this argument, De Grauwe says that for him, inflation targeting is an unnecessary mechanism to try to influence asset prices. He says that if the banking system were isolated from asset markets, then the crisis would affect only the nonbanking sector and, in this way, ensure the liquidity of the market.

The problem in the recent crisis was that commercial banks were both highly involved in the development of the housing bubble and the subsequent crisis. Given that the banking system was highly correlated with the price of assets, the central bank was heavily involved with the banks since the issuing institution should serve as the lender of last resort. Economic theory says that central banks should intervene by providing the economy with liquidity when the lack of the latter significantly alters the system of payments and, as a result, private agents.[9]

So that the detection of bubbles by issuing institutions is of vital importance, since the event that follows it is usually a crisis. It is at this time that the balance sheets of the Central Bank are inevitably affected and the reason why they sometimes choose to "do nothing," although there are costs arising from the involvement of their balance sheets. There is one reason why the policy of "nonintervention" is the desired option. During recent years, there has been an important role of the creation of liquidity and credit outside the banking system. Hedge funds, both short- and long-term ones, had been provided, which led to the creation of credit and massive liquidity schemes to elude regulation and supervision.[10]

De Grauwe argues that the central bank would expand insurance of liquidity for certain institutions that were outside its regulatory framework and that this is not reasonable. Also, for De Grauwe (2007), "asset bubbles are a relevant issue and that once it has detected one, should be attacked". He continues to say that it is not credible that no bubble can be detected; "one should be blind not to see a bubble" (De Grauwe, 2007), especially when the price of particular industry assets grow at a rate of 20% or more, then, the aggregate credit is increased by a similar percentage for several years and could, therefore, be indicative that it is managing a bubble and that a crisis is imminent.

---

[9]Central banks are forced to provide liquidity in some way to the economy when a crisis arises since these bodies are the only ones qualified to do so.

[10]While this liquidity does not cause problems for the banks, it then does not cause any concern or occupation to the central bank.

In addition, it is considered that central banks can identify bubbles and, if they are capable of controlling inflation, then they should be able to stop the processes of generation of asset bubbles. De Grauwe recommended that central banks be more closely involved in the regulation of all institutions creating credit and liquidity. Finally, he concludes that the IT is just an imposition of fashion and that it is a position whose main feature is to restrict the activities of the central bank to ensure price stability when, from his perspective, it is able to engage in the prevention of bubbles and the monitoring of those institutions that are in the business of creating credit and liquidity.

For their part, writers such as Calvo and Mendoza (1999a, 2001, 2002) are skeptical that inflation targeting can serve as a strategy of monetary policy in emerging countries. These authors based their concern on the fact that allowing high level of discretion to those responsible for implementing monetary policy with too weak institutions can lead to poor macroeconomic performance due, essentially, to the lack of credibility and low reputation of these institutions, this problem, in some way, is observed in developed countries.

The diversity of discussions regarding inflation targeting highlights the concern voiced by the main central bank of the planet – one headed by the Chairman of the Federal Reserve System (FED), Bernanke[11] and Kohn, Vice-Chairman of the Board of Governors, main advisor, and operator of the management of Alan Greenspan at the head of the FED. The first based his argument that the FED has built and increased its degree of credibility by the fight against inflation and that credibility has provided to the issuing institution relative flexibility to disturbances of short-term product and employment without destabilizing inflation expectations.

In addition, Bernanke is convinced that when the economy is operating with price stability, the expectations and public beliefs about the plans of the central bank are improved significantly. If the public is not convinced that the central bank prefers a low inflation, expectations regarding future actions become highly sensitive and, therefore, injects uncertainty about the level of inflation that the central banker seeks, which can lead to greater economic and financial uncertainty.

On the premise of the communication, the Chairman of the FED establishes that incremental movements through the target of inflation, in

---

[11]He joined the Federal Reserve System as one of the Governors in 2002. He is convinced that if the economic players know the rules and mechanisms that the central bank uses, the markets operate more efficiently.

the form of long-term goal, could help the US central bank to have greater communication and "perhaps" to improve policy decisions without the fear of the cost relating to the potential loss of flexibility. Then, Bernanke (2003) defined optimal long-run inflation rate (OLIR) as the "inflation which achieves the best average economic performance over time in terms of inflation and unemployment objectives".

For the dual mandate, the OLIR is the relevant concept in the field of central banks. This does not necessarily mean that the inflation rate is equivalent to price stability. Thus, under a dual regime, the benefits of reducing microeconomic disturbances arising from price stability are overcome by the cost of the very common situations in which nominal federal funds rates are zero. "Therefore, the OLIR must be greater than zero but correctly measured" (Bernanke, 2003).[12] Finally, Bernanke says that announcing the OLIR does not represent any problem regarding an excessive restriction of short-term monetary policy. Therefore, to reassure those concerns about the potential loss of flexibility, it is required that the Federal Open Market Committee (FOMC) announces the OLIR with the following features to audiences.

i) Keep the rate of inflation at its steady state and preserve it on aver-age over the economic cycle level.

ii) The FOMC must always take into account the implications for short-term economic and financial stability.

For his part, Donald Kohn[13] calls himself a skeptic of the inflation targeting and puts in doubt that inflation targeting has been useful in various episodes of the monetary policy of the USA. He agrees with advocates of the targets of inflation in many critical areas that *price stability* is the primary objective of long-term monetary policy.[14] In some countries, the adoption of inflation targeting in conjunction with the independence of the central bank and the initiation of the use of IT has represented a big step for the pursuit of price stability.

The question that Kohn wants to resolve is whether inflation targeting contributes to improvement of economic performance in the USA. That is, if the targets of inflation lead to actions of private agents and policymak-

---

[12]Then, the OLIR should be lower than the inflation rate, i.e., one in which the risks of the federal funds rate to reach the zero bound are minimized.

[13]Donald Lewis Kohn joined as Vice President of the Board of Governors and as chief adviser and operator of the management of Alan Greenspan at the head of the FED. Kohn set arguments against the rule of Taylor and that the Federal Reserve does not implement inflation-targeting approach strictly.

[14]In the words of Kohn, achieving price stability is the best way in which the policy can contribute to the well-being of a country.

ers to increase the chances of keeping production of the economy to its maximum sustainable level with a low and stable inflation rate. Response to Kohn is not proven and possibly negative, at least for us, and may even interfere in the economy in the medium and long terms.

Kohn based his arguments on the premise that the USA carried out a successful monetary policy over the past 2 decades. The FED has been able to achieve price stability, "the expectations are low and stable" (Kohn, 2003), and this happened with a couple of mild recessions. However, from his perspective, many diverse factors have contributed to the above, including monetary policy. Therefore, for Kohn, the best choice is to continue to do what the Federal Reserve has been doing and has recommended maintaining the *status quo*.

The former Vice President of the Board of Governors of the FED believes that the adoption of inflation targeting, even in its simplest version, throws benefits that do not exceed their costs. A gain in respect of costs is that, under certain circumstances, central bankers face *trade-offs* between economic stability and short-term inflation stability and, therefore, considers that the implementation of inflation targeting could be less than optimal with respect to the stabilization of the economy and financial markets.[15],[16]

Also, we do not see any convincing evidence that economies that use targets for price controls have lower or more stable inflation rates or that its result will be more stable around its potential (or the target). Therefore, it appears that inflation targeting produces only a slight or no improvement in the variable target. Regarding communication and transparency, says Kohn, in practice, the targets of inflation do not mention the time periods in which there will be variations to the stability of prices and, much less, the reasons why the variations mentioned will succeed.

For his part, Broaddus[17] recognizes that the introduction of explicit inflation targeting generates questions and doubts about exactly what its operational role is in the implementation of monetary policy. In addition, the above can be achieved without overly restricting traditional policies of

---

[15]It is clear that from the point of view of Kohn, the FED has operated to reduce the instability of prices in the US economy without the application of targets of inflation or by a target implicit in the structure of monetary policy.

[16]Kohn argues that the US economy has benefited from the flexibility that the FED succeeded in abandoning a formal inflation target. He defines flexibility not as little frequent changes in long-term goals but as freedom of moving away from price stability in the long term, only for a period of time. He affirms that this type of flexibility is possible in different models of inflation targeting but doubted its effectiveness in practice.

[17]In 2003, he was the President of the Federal Reserve Bank of Richmond.

stabilization of long term of the FOMC. So, Broaddus says that, indeed, a target of inflation is not limited to the FED for taking action in policies practiced by them to stabilize employment and product. What Broaddus wanted to emphasize is that inflation targeting helps to discipline and to justify the decisions of central bankers aimed to stabilize the product, employment, and to "protect the purchasing power of the currency" (Broaddus, 2004).

KEYWORDS

- **Monetary policy**
- **Keynesian**
- **Escape clause**
- **Institutional environment,**
- **Operational framework,**
- **Transparency policy**

CHAPTER 3

POLICY RULES

CONTENTS

Our economic system will work best when producers and consumers, employers and employees, can proceed with full confidence that the average level of prices will behave in a known way in the future—preferably that it will be highly stable.
—Milton Friedman, 1968

The phenomenon of inflation has been breaking down successfully in the past 30 years, from very high rates of inflation to moderate figures. In general, price and product stability has been obtained (with the exception of the process resulting from the recent *subprime* crisis). There is a direct causal connection between changes in monetary policy and the improvement of economic performance indicators (Taylor, 2005). In general, in terms of the definition of price stability as the main goal of the central banks, inflationary processes have been minor and have been reduced through the use of their instruments in a systematic way.[1]

It suggests, therefore, that efforts should be concentrated on the stability of prices due to the benefits achieved until the year 2005. Then, inflation control at a low and stable level ensures that private actors with endurance generate expectations of macroeconomic stability. In practice, and to achieve the above, it is necessary to determine an instrument.[2] Recently, the variable decision that most central banks use is the interest rate.[3]

The traditional policies of the central bank *leaning against the wind* could be understood as an effort of the central banker to apply some systematic component to the fundamental of their decisions. Therefore, they *could be* understood as such since they make varying monetary aggregates

---

[1]An element additional to consider is that through this set of policy measures, in the words of Taylor, the cycles of economic expansion have lengthened and recessions have been milder and less frequent.
[2]Some classic authors such as Smith considered that regulation in paper money may represent an improvement of economic performance (stability and growth). Since then, leading economic thinkers have acknowledged the importance of systematic mechanisms that regulate the behavior of government entities. Subsequently, at the beginning of the nineteenth century, Thornton and then Ricardo established the importance of the one "guide rule" of monetary policy once empirical evidence is obtained: "The Napoleonic wars led to financial crises arising from the increase of liquidity to finance military projects" (Taylor and Williams, 2010).

The effects of the Second World War propelled authors such as Fisher and Wicksell to propose policy rules to prevent "monetary excesses" that led to hyperinflationary processes. However, Friedman made the rule of "steady growth," after reviewing the actions undertaken during and after the great depression.
[3]Although a monetary aggregate (monetary base) serves this role in some cases. Taylor has focused on rules based on monetary aggregates but, from 1985, concentrated on those that have the interest rate as a mechanism because they work better in general except in extreme situations (very high inflation or deflation).

or interest rates, as the case may be.[4] However, although variations of the money supply or interest rate processes can be identified when there are inflationary pressures, it is not possible to determine what causes such pressure, how it can be measured, and how much one should modify the instruments. Such policies therefore lack content and structure by what cannot be taken as rules of monetary policy.

In addition, it is essential to consider the role of expectations of future instruments of policy changes since they have large effects on the economy in general. Therefore, specifying in detail the way in which monetary authorities will act to certain variations and the proportions in which they modify their instruments turns out to be essential to have a "good" systematic component of monetary policy.[5]

3.1 ORIGINS

A common problem facing a policymaker is the dilemma between the two options: operating under the application of the rules or altering them (discretion) in order to obtain certain effects in their favor. However, discretion does not always bring positive results in terms of the variables that occupy the economic authorities or the efforts of policymakers. For starters, discretion is an advantage for any authority. It, in effect, gives flexibility to performance and allows one to have a wide range of evidence, i.e., recent information, for decision making.

The rules were set forth earlier ($t_n - 1$) and, therefore, with a set of more limited information, which the authority has at the time, they adopt specific decisions. In this sense, rules impose obstacles to economic policymakers in doing what they think is the optimal course at a given moment. However, this does not mean that discretion is better than the application of rules (Taylor, 1999); the working paper on policy rule defines discretion as follows:

...a contingency plan that specifies as clearly as possible the circumstances under which a central bank should change the monetary policy instruments.

In this way, and under certain circumstances, the application of rules is preferable for different reasons. Two are herein presented. One refers to the idiosyncratic nature of the economic authorities. Theories and models of

---

[4]This can be interpreted as "a contingency plan" similar to a policy rule.
[5]Mishkin refers to these needs as possible actions of "irresponsible" authorities.

economic(s) suppose policymakers as consistent and over time (dynamic). In practice, however, the economic authority is a large and heterogeneous set of institutions and personalities who interact among themselves, which change frequently and have different interests and objectives. In this context, the existence of rules can contribute to the scenario that decisions are within a reasonable range in terms of its contribution to social welfare.

The second reason refers to signals to the private sector and which constitute the conditions so that the latter determine their decisions. That is, according to the objectives set by economic policymakers, private agents such as businesses and families determine their strategies, which under these conditions are optimal for the performance of companies and families. Similarly, cooperation between authorities and private agents is determined by the commitment of the latter to maintain this stance before any internal and external situation. However, there are also benefits under a discretionary regime.

Previously, the objective of monetary authorities was reflected in the preferences and needs of the most representative private agents. Now, this objective is expressed as a function of the current and expected levels of inflation. On a discretionary basis, the monetary authority can print more money and create more inflation than people expect. This results in two phenomena to be considered:
  i)   Expansion of economic activity and
  ii) Reductions in the real value of nominal liabilities of Government (Barro and Gordon, 1983).

However, these surprises and their resulting benefits may not be systematically operating or balanced. This means that the use of surprise inflation as an instrument of economic growth only brings benefits in the period "$t + 1$," which means that prices steadily rise and would imply higher social costs than benefits in "$t + 2$." In this sense, people adjust their expectations of inflation to eliminate the surprise pattern.

Now, when there are rules, monetary policymakers are *tempted* to cheat (operated by restricted discretion) in each period with the aim of obtaining benefits provided by *inflationary* shocks. However, this tendency to deceive threatens the viability of the standards of balance and tends to move the economy toward lower balances due to the discretion policy.

It is also said that due to the fact that those responsible for implementing policy and private agents interact on an ongoing basis; it is possible that the first to dip into the reputation or credibility give support to the application of rules (discretion). This causes the possible loss of credibility, forcing central bankers to comply with standards, so "some policy rules can necessarily be performed by the possibility of a potential loss of reputation or credibility by policymakers" (Barro and Gordon, 1983).

Then, surprise inflation benefits arise when the rate of inflation in the period (π_t) exceeds the expected level (π_t^e). Therefore, an unexpected monetary expansion is reflected in positive values for ($\pi_t - \pi_t^e$), resulting in an increase in economic activity. Equivalently, these nominal shocks make unemployment level to decrease below the natural rate.[6] This natural rate can change over time due to movements of supply, demographic changes, and changes in fiscal policy and programs (subsidies).

Other benefits generated by surprise inflation lie in government revenue, i.e., in the "consequences" of inflationary finance. This means that inflation expectations (formed in the previous period) determine the necessary amount of money (cash) of the population. When the inflationary surprise is greater (observed – expected), effectively depreciating the real value of money, it allows the Government to "create" new money in real terms. The policymaker evaluates the possibility of applying the above as a replacement of a tax such as the income tax. Therefore, the inflation benefits depend on externalities.

Another way in which surprise inflation generates revenue for the Government is when people keep the amount of government bonds in advance. Bonds are charged with the actual performance, which is satisfactory to the expectation of inflation of people. However, surprise inflation depreciates part of the real value of the bonds, which in turn, reduces future payments from the Government in respect of interest and principal payment.

So, to minimize the expected costs, agents use the observed inflation data. People predict inflation with rational expectations, while the objective of policymakers is $\pi^e = \pi_{\text{forecast}}$. Therefore, the central bank may condition the inflation rate through variables that are also known to private agents.

Then, the central banker chooses the "observed" and "expected" data of inflation together under the so-called condition that they "are the same." In this way, Barth argues that the best *standard prescribes zero at all the inflation*. The central point is that under rules, costs are lower than those obtained under discretion. The lower costs are reflected in the ability to

---

[6]The natural rate of unemployment occurs when the difference between π_t and π_t^e is zero.

make commitments and contractual agreements between private actors and agencies responsible for implementing monetary policy.

In this way, if the issuing institution wants to mislead the public by surprise inflation, it will induce the increase of the product and employment above the natural rate. But, if agents act with rational expectations and if the central bank's action is announced (discretionary), the authorities will not be able to mislead the public. In this sense, the variation of rise in the inflation rate does not bring benefits.

In addition, a good monetary policy rule is one in which the fluctuations of current inflation with respect to its objective are small. More specific the rule, greater is the achieved transparency although there are factors that are not included in the policy rule, such as the liquidity crisis in financial markets, forcing the central banks to modify the rate of interest (discretion). When monetary policy use of the concept of policy rule is analyzed, it is necessary to distinguish between "changes in the instruments of monetary policy due to changes in the policy rule and changes in monetary policy instruments caused by movements along the policy rule" (Taylor, 2003).

Taylor says that the equation for the amount of money, proposed by Friedman and Schwartz (1963), was useful both for the period of the gold and the dollar as standard and for the period when it exists and when there is no central bank.

The equation for the amount of money ($MV = PY$) was used to determine monetary policy; however, Taylor analysis requires a different equation, i.e., a rule for monetary policy in which short-term interest rate is a function of the rate of inflation and real gross domestic product (GDP). Obviously, the monetary policy of the Taylor rule equation differs from the amount of money of the Friedman equation; however, these are connected, since the first can be derived from the second.

To derive a rule for monetary policy for the equation for the amount of money, it is necessary to assume the following:

i)   The money supply is fixed or growing at a constant rate.
ii) Now, knowing that the speed depends on the rate of interest (r) and the product (Y), it can be replaced by V in the equation of the amount of money. There is a relationship between (r), (P), and (Y).
iii) Finally, (r) on the left side is cleared and the interest rate is obtained as a function of the level of prices and the actual product.

It is important to note that this function relates the rate of interest with real output and the price level. The functional form used by Taylor is linear for the interest rate and logarithmic for the level of prices and real output. These last two variables consider the variation of the actual product of a possible stochastic trend and consider that the first logarithm of price level differences is stationary.

$$r = \pi + gy + h\left(\pi - \pi^*\right) + r^f, \tag{3.1}$$

where $r=$ is the short-term interest rate, $\pi =$ is the rate of inflation (percentage change in P), and $y=$ is the percentage deviation of the actual product (Y), a tendency. The variables g, h, π^*, y, and r^f are constant.

Equation (3.1) is used to describe monetary policy in different periods of time when there are different policy regimes. This equation can represent a guide or a strict formula for decision making related to monetary policy by the central bank. Now, if the policy rules to increase the interest rate, then, e.g., the *Federal Open Market Committee* (FOMC) could carry out open market sales operations and thereby adjust money supply appropriately for such an increase of the interest rate.

In this case, the parameters of equation (3.1) have the following interpretation:

π^* : is the target of the inflation rate;

r^f : is the estimated equilibrium real interest rate of the central bank;

h: represents the value by which the *Federal Reserve* System (FED) increases the real interest rate *ex post* $(r - \pi)$ in response to an increase in inflation; and

g : is the value by which the FED changes the real interest rate upward in response to an increase in inflation.

For the particular case of

$g = 0.5, \pi^* = 2y,$

$==h = 0.5, \ r^f = 2.$

Equation (3.1) is precisely derived in the way suggested by Taylor (1993).

As mentioned earlier, the use of policy rules was begun to delimit the powers of the authorities and governments, i.e., to avoid discretionary actions. However, the development of new mechanisms to limit the degree of interference of these entities on key aspects of the economy, including inflation-targeting approach, has granted some freedom in its management. In this context, the option of using the money supply as a key instrument of policy rules rather than as a rule allows a smooth growth of money and credit, such as that proposed by Friedman (1963).

The evolution of monetary policy rules can be understood as a gradual process in which FED learned to conduct monetary policy. This learning was the result of research conducted by the same FED, criticisms of monetary economists outside it, through observations of the behavior of the issuing institutions in other countries, and through personal experience of the members of the FOMC (Taylor, 1999).

Therefore, policy rules arise from classic perception, which adds power to the State. In the modern version, Friedman proposed a rule of k%, which consists in that the more efficient monetary aggregate should grow as a "certain percentage," roughly equal to the nominal GDP trend. In this way, Friedman proposed rules while the new Keynesians suggested to "calibrate" the variables as appropriate, i.e., discretion.

In addition, the Taylor rule has a series of requirements that are presented below.

i)   *Natural rate of unemployment (Friedman, 1968)*: This is the rate at which the economy is going to remain in the long term and is independent of the behavior of prices.

Corollary. Accelerationist hypothesis: there is a *trade-off* between unemployment and upward inflation gap. Since this exchange does not come from the observed inflation, if inflation is not anticipated, it is result of the acceptance of the natural rate of unemployment. The *trade-off* between unemployment and prices only exists in the short term.[7]

i)   *Rational expectations hypothesis (Muth, 1961)*: This comprises predictions informed of future events. It is considered that all individuals take into account all available information at their disposal and therefore agents incur no systematic errors on average and do not commit errors.

Recognition of rational expectations does not imply that monetary policy is ineffective. This means the rejection of the proposition of ineffectiveness of Sargent–Wallace–Taylor.

i)   *Dynamic inconsistency (Kydland and Prescott, 1977)*: A policy that is consistent is selected as the best option for each period (this implies discretion) given the current economic situation.

---

[7]For the economy to be placed in a general state of excess demand, it will be required to accelerate inflation continually to maintain this situation.

ii) *Advantage of cooperative games (Barro and Gordon, 1983)*: This theory proposes that selection involving "it is better," given the current situation, not the maximization of the social objective function. Therefore, discretion costs are greater than the (credibility) rules.

- The demonstration of dynamic inconsistency assumes the superiority of discretion policy rules.
- Credibility has empirically significant benefits.

Credibility is equivalent, in game theory, to cooperative solutions (balances of reputation). The cooperative solutions are consistent dynamically, since agents rank their decisions since they believe the Government.

i) *The Taylor curve (1979)*: Because the Phillips curve had ceased to be used for economic analysis and, therefore, economic policy because of the *trade-offs* between inflation and unemployment, short runs ceased to exist. Taylor discovered that such *trade-offs* already persisted not between the described or tiered variables, but that now, short-term exchanges are recorded between variability and prices and product. This new relationship was called the second-order Phillips curve by Taylor, but shortly afterward, it was called the Taylor curve.

ii) *Invalidity of the proposition of ineffectiveness (1975)*: In response to the variances problem posed by the Taylor curve, a systematic mechanism that controls and stabilizes the problem of such variations, the Taylor rule, was developed, which was designed in a context of econometric modeling.

iii) *The criticism of Lucas (1976)*: Econometric evaluation of the rules of monetary and fiscal policy using macroeconomic methods of rational expectations has been motivated by many factors. The substance of criticism of Lucas is that the evaluation of policies through traditional econometrics is defective, since recognition of rational expectations does not imply that monetary policy is ineffective.[8] Lucas (1976) argues that "characteristics that lead to success in short term prognosis are not related to the quantitative evaluation of the policy".

Most of the econometric models are designed for play characteristics (short-term forecasts); however, the use of these models does not provide

---

[8]For Lucas, traditional econometrics, or as he calls it "the theory of monetary policy," which is based on such tradition, requires a better review.

useful information regarding the actual consequences of economic policy alternatives.[9]

3.1.1   TAYLOR RULE

This rule was originally designed for the US economy, and is necessary to mention, that there is a loss function that considers a target for inflation and a value for the product behind the Taylor rule, who generate the economy by no monetary circumstances. In addition, he ponders the penalty in every deviation from the product and inflation.

$$\gamma(y_t - y_t^n)^2 + (1 - \gamma)(\pi_t - \pi^T)^2 = 0, \qquad (3.2)$$

where $\gamma \in [0,1]$ and indicates how the authorities react when variables are far from their targets. To find the optimal monetary rule from the loss function, an optimization process that minimizes the fluctuations is carried out.

The analysis proposed initially for the USA was expanded to create a model for several countries (the seven most industrialized economies). Taylor used a multinational econometric model with rational expectations in which different policy rules were analyzed in a context of international interaction. Taylor made an evaluation with fixed exchange rate regime and after with flexible exchange rate in his work of 1979, and then he classified according to what was successful in terms of stability of prices and product.

In addition, there was greater independence for central banks in the management of monetary policy with a flexible exchange rate regime. This model includes the expectations by introducing the assumption of rational expectations, whose results showed that the fluctuations in real output are higher when the exchange rate is fixed. The foregoing derives the conclusion that central banks should pay little attention to the exchange rate and should focus on controlling inflation in product variations.

In the model of several countries, the interest rate on the short term rather than the money supply is used as the main policy instrument. This

---

[9]An additional vein of the Lucas critique on the case study of prolonged inflation, completely based on econometric simulations, is now being addressed more seriously than he had enjoyed for decades. Therefore, Lucas's theory is not only appropriate but necessary to review the scientific basis of its reasoning again.

is due to the fact that Taylor considered that in this way, the model adheres more to the way in which central bank's monetary policy is formed. Rule was calculated empirically for the European Union (EU) and special emphasis was laid on the fact that "there is no consensus on the size of the coefficients of the rules" (Taylor, 1993). Therefore, the coefficients and the targets originally designed cannot be used for all economies.

The original nonobviousness rules mandate that organizations must follow the FED.[10] This rule, by definition, is a hierarchical rule.

$$r = P + 0.5y + 0.5(P - 2) + 2, \tag{3.3}$$

where r: Federal funds rate, P: inflation rate of the previous four quarters, and Y: percentage deviation of real GDP; in other words, Y: real GDP and Y^*: is a trend of real GDP.

It is important to clarify that the federal funds rate is the instrumental variable in the United States case; however, for other countries, the key variable is the interbank interest rate. In this way is exemplified the way in which central banks, acting through rules, try to manipulate a nominal variable to affect a real variable and other nominal variables.[11] The above shows one of the main objections to the use of rules, i.e., the "nonobservability" of variables. The variables involved here are *i*) potential GDP, *ii*) the equilibrium real interest rate, and *iii*) expected inflation rate.

Therefore, the specificity of the rule is that "the quarterly average federal funds rate must grow 1.5 times to an increase of one percentage unit of the quarterly average inflation rate or 0.5 times to an increase of the same magnitude of the output gap" (Taylor, 1993).

Finally, it is necessary and appropriate to establish that (r), the short-term interest rate, is determined by the market, so the central bank intervenes indirectly in the bond market by suggesting a reference rate. This interest rate is crucial and the central bank should identify it to differentiate it from country to country, but its function is the same in different countries. Regarding the value of the coefficients, depending on how the economy is humming, the central bank looks for the value that minimizes the variability of inflation and the product.

---

[10]The mandate of central banking is denoted in the loss function, where if $\gamma = 0.5$, then the mandate will be dual. It can also be hierarchical or unique, with $\gamma = 0.2$ (for example) or $\gamma = 0$, respectively.
[11]Supporters of the rule argue that it is possible to do the above, although control of the nominal variable (on the right side of the equation) can impact on the performance of the real variable (located on the side of equality).

3.2 EVOLUTION

The use of rules stems from the debate between rules and discretion, i.e., the temptation that makes policymakers "cheats" for private actors to benefit in the short term at the cost of loss of credibility and reputation. In this way, it is necessary to define what a rule of policy and a discretionary policy are.

Policy rule: is a preagreed intervention to a problem of dynamic optimization. It can also be defined as a contingency plan that specifies as clearly as possible the circumstances under which a central bank should change the monetary policy instruments.

The superiority of the discretion rules should be recognized. Today, when the coefficients of a rule are not adequate to deal with supply shocks, the central bankers consider the act of discretion (Barro and Gordon, 1983). It is for this reason that the policy rules have functioned as a mechanism that restricts, in some way, the power to the State and, in the modern version; Friedman was a pioneer in proposing them as such.

Taylor reviewed the proposals of Friedman and considered that the application of rules was not wrong and argues that "a monetary policy rule is better than another if it generate an improved economic performance according to any criteria" (Taylor, 1999). Therefore, no monetary theory is able to provide a fully reliable guide of what will happen in the future. Thus, for the evaluation of monetary policy (such as that in Taylor, 1993) rules, it was necessary to introduce some assumptions. The main among them is the acceptance of rational expectations. Thereby, there are two types of rules:

  i)   The *rigid rules* (no feedback) are those that do not consider the State of the world to make decisions; among them, is the rule of constant growth of Milton Friedman.

  ii) The *flexible rules* (with feedback): are mechanisms that capture the state of the world for decision making in their formulation. The flexible rules include monetary aggregate (McCallum rule) rules and the rules of rate of interest (Taylor rule).

Two main types are distinguished within the flexible rules:

  i)   *Rules of monetary aggregates*: the evolution and behavior of the monetary aggregate involves allowing the central bank to indicate its position.

  ii) *Interest rate rules*: are used to set the interest rate, either upward or downward as the case may be, as an instrument of monetary policy by the central bank to achieve the set of objectives. And these can be of the following types: original, inertial, prognosis, etc.

Given that the Taylor rule assumes rational expectations, the application of the Taylor rule is situated in a dynamic game, where the supremacy of the cooperative solutions over noncooperative solutions is evident; this means that the rules on discretionary policy are supported.[12] He also stated that, in the long term, the implementation and monitoring of a policy rule yields good results, while deviations from this rule bring benefits only in the short term, such as those proposed by Barro and Gordon (1983).

It is clear that some rules, from their conception, assume the possibility of deviations in their implementation. In this case, the original Taylor rule has in its structure the concept of dynamic inconsistency, proposed by Kydland and Prescott (1977),[13] and Taylor being a rule with feedback, such deviations from the objectives can be considered consistent, since you choose a certain alternative depending on the current state of the economy.

On the other hand, Taylor says that the fact that the rules of monetary policy can be expressed as mathematical equations, seemingly mechanical, does not imply that central banks should implement them as formulas. Most of the proposed monetary policy rules suggest that they should be used as guides of general structures of policy. In this way, the mathematical form of the rule becomes "average approximation," now that some degree of discretion is necessary to implement the policy rule.

The use of the Taylor rule in econometric models generated upgrades such as those observed in Taylor (1999b). The use of monetary rules adopted different assumptions (stochastic, dynamic, and general equilibrium models). The work of Taylor (1999b) held the following assumptions:
  i)   Rational expectations;
  ii) Sticky prices, overlapping wages; and
  iii) A transmission mechanism of monetary policy with a "vision of financial market." This considers the effects that monetary policy has on financial assets possessed by the public, which, therefore, affect consumption decisions.

In the model of several countries, it was found that it is relevant to include exchange rate in the rule; however, Taylor (1993b) believes that its

---

[12]This tendency to deceive threatens the viability of the standards of balance and tends to move the economy toward lower balances due to the discretion policy.
[13]If agents are rational and the criticism of Lucas is true, then it is preferable to submit to policy rules in the long run than to discretionary policies because this type of policy tends to be suboptimal in the long term.

inclusion "would affect inflation and the product", so setting a target for inflation is enough and that there is no need to react to changes in the exchange rate. Another application of the Taylor rule is to analyze the probability that the problem of having a nominal interest rate equal or close to zero arises.

Economists like Orphanides, Fuhrer, King, etc., in their investigations, concluded that "If monetary policy is in accordance with the policy rule, it is unlikely to register an interest rate close to zero" (Taylor, 2000a). Subsequently, Taylor (2009) shows evidence of the consequences of the abandonment of the rule, as the worst of its effects, including the recent financial crisis with a nominal rate close to zero.

Taylor confirms that monetary and fiscal policy had a defining role before, during, and after the financial crisis, manifesting itself in macroeconomic policies that do not take us to the right path. It is considered that monetary policy deviated from a process that had held for two decades by less interventionism, i.e., with actions increasingly based on rules that led to higher moderation. The abandonment of these precepts (great deviation) led the economy to the great recession and the recession of 2009. Thus, Taylor used relevant information, and using statistical techniques, he tried to establish policy.

John Taylor established that since the late 1940s, up to the beginning of the decade of the eighties, the real GDP registered a clearly volatile behavior. From the point of view of the monetary policy rule of the type most commonly used by central banks, the beginning of a prolonged period of stability of US real output was seen at the start of the 1982 expansion and it initiated a process called the great moderation. In this period, the variability not only of the product but also of indicators such as inflation and US interest rates fell sharply. This was essentially due to the implementation of monetary policy rules by the authorities of the country.

According to Taylor (2010), the great moderation was completed due to the great diversion, in which, "economic policy has turned in a different sense from that which had worked well during the great moderation". Therefore, when such deviation occurred, economic performance began to deteriorate and led to greater fluctuation processes of fundamental variables and, consequently, a considerable increase of uncertainty in different markets. The hypothesis of great deviation indicates that a set of misguided monetary policies by the FED generated the crisis. The main elements of this approach are as follows.

The economic crisis arose years ago, in the period from 2002 to 2005, when policy decisions of the Federal Reserve, in terms of its target for the federal funds rate, were very much below that recommended by the Taylor rule. The monetary stance, excessively relaxed during these years, accelerated the *boom* in the housing sector, which generated strong financial pressures in the USA and other countries, which then burst and created the crisis.

This situation led to decisions on low rates of interest in the USA to have influence over decreases in the rates in various countries, which represented a global interaction between central banks that caused lower-than-expected interest rates. Those countries that most deviated from the Taylor rule underwent more dynamism in their housing sector. So, this fact could establish a direct relationship between the size of the deviation from the rule and the experienced mortgage *boom*.[14] However, for Taylor, this result did not surprise him, since it is evident that an unusual policy usually causes problems.

According to Taylor, very low interest rates served as catalysts for the *boom* in the housing sector, which in turn led to risk-taking in housing finance processes and, eventually, to an increase in mortgage defaults and the deterioration of financial institutions' balance sheets. To demonstrate the connection between low interest rates and the housing *boom*, Taylor made use of a model that related the rate of federal funds to the construction of houses. This counterfactual model showed that higher federal fund interest rates did not cause a *boom* in the housing sector.

Taylor called this a discretionary monetary policy decision, because the Government intervenes to stop implementing policies that are being systematically used. Curious is the way that Taylor has to express his point of view since it recognizes that despite what it caused and although it could have been avoided by using its monetary policy rule,[15] the Federal Reserve acted in well-intentioned manner using modulated discretion. Therefore, it is evident that Taylor disagrees and more or less accepted the proposition of the Greenspan–Kohn approach concerning the origin of the financial crisis.[16]

---

[14] Interest rates were so low that the real interest rate was negative for a very long period of time.

[15] Through the application of small variations according to the needs and opportunities of monetary policy.

[16] Another wrong answer was the drastic reduction in the federal funds rate. The objective step of 5.25% from mid-2007 to 2.00% in April 2008 prompted a sharp depreciation of the dollar and a huge increase in the prices of oil and other *commodities*, hitting the economy and prolonging the crisis.

Taylor, unlike Greenspan and Kohn, certifies that the epicenter of the financial crisis was the product of a deviation from policy, while the latter two propose a deregulated and almost unmonitored enveloping process of diversification of financial instruments, backed by subprime mortgages, essentially derived from an excess of savings in underdeveloped countries, which was oriented toward industrialized countries. In this way, this deviation was perceived by the markets, causing considerable uncertainty in the environment, and then the exclusion of policy rules confirmed the uncertainty that soon turned into panic.[17]

An additional extension is the application of the rule in emerging economies (EU), where it is crucial to make an appropriate selection of the instrument of monetary policy. If there is uncertainty in the actual measurement of the rate of interest, significant shocks to investment or exports, and difficulty to measure the equilibrium real interest rate, it is recommended to make use of an instrument of monetary aggregates. The use of monetary aggregates is suggested because in these economies, strong inflationary processes that make it difficult for the measurement of the real rate of interest are recorded. On the other hand, "If the speed of impact is large, the interest rate is recommended" (Taylor, 2000).

The authorities should be sufficiently clear about their actions and intentions and must maintain a rule for long time periods, so agents can form their expectations. In emerging economies, best results are dumped if one takes into account the variable "type of change within the rule." Svensson and Ball found that the rule performance is improved by considering the type of change in small economies. The inclusion of the exchange rate variable into the structure of the type of Taylor rule aims to counteract the effects of contractionary appreciation via the stimulation of aggregate demand. Therefore, the specificity of the rule with respect to the exchange rate is considering "If a domestic currency appreciation occurs, it would lead to a reduction in the interest rate" (Taylor, 2001).

3.3   DEVELOPMENTS AND CONTROVERSIES

Most of the central banks of the world have consensus regarding the use of rules as a reference (benchmark) for the formation of policy. However, there is no complete acceptance of the use of rules in the FED, since the

---

[17]In addition, Taylor argues that the crisis was misdiagnosed as a problem of liquidity, so the policies did not attack the problem.

discussion is still in the rules versus discretion debate. This is precisely because the course based on the Taylor rule is not rigid, since it allows a degree of flexibility to unforeseen events and, therefore, is not to be followed mechanically, but as a reference for policymakers. The current President of the US Central Bank has a stance in favor of rules, flexible or bounded rules at its discretion, as did Taylor.

The rules against discretion debate has been maintained since the use of rules should be understood as a frame of reference for monetary policy decision making rather than being assumed as mathematical formulas. Given the above, there are controversies around the use of rules, and this work will focus on those relating to the problems of measurement. Measurement issues have to do with the use of past information and some of the variables included in the rule are not observable.

On the other hand, this refers to another kind of objection to the way in which the rule is calculated, i.e., somehow, both variables and coefficients of the same changes have become arbitrary. One of the main players in this debate is Athanasios Orphanides, Governor of the Central Bank of Cyprus during the period 2007–2012. Knowing the above, the work of Orphanides (2003) says that the Taylor rule is based on a little Royal course; he argues that it is difficult to obtain data in a timely manner: this means that the variables involved are known accurately only after time has elapsed. This may mean that, using this type of information, rule does not describe correctly the behavior of the central bank. Orphanides also argues that US policy mistakes in the decade of the 1970s could have been caused by higher estimates of GDP.

Once the relationship between policy rules and inflation targeting (see Chapter 2) is raised, one could argue the need for discretion in the *tripod* posed by Taylor since the inflation-targeting scheme allows the possibility of the use of ranges and because the rules should not be followed mechanically, but as a reference. The above inserts uncertainty and imposes a degree of uncertainty for the private agents when making decisions. Despite this, these ranges give flexibility to short-term monetary policymakers.

Specifically, the rules referred to these critical issues[18]:

---

[18]It is appropriate to survey the tenor of some other criticisms of the use of rules: i) giving the same weight to the inflation gap and product does not always yield the best result, ii) the target of inflation of 2% could be too restrictive (in the US case), iii) lack of transparency of the central bank, and iv) rule reacts to changes in real variables such as product. The argument for this is that monetary policy has no effect in the long run on this type of variables.

i)   "It is difficult to accurately determine the potential product that will be set as a target in the rule" (Taylor, 2003). It is difficult in practice for the implementation of the policy if the measurements of the variables of interest, e.g., both the equilibrium real interest rate and the output gap, are unobservable variables.

ii) A bad estimate of the equilibrium real rate would become a calculated evil, the price level, and therefore a biased definition of the instrument of monetary policy (in the case of US federal funds rate).

In this regard, Taylor (2003) says that the precise or approximate calculation of potential GDP is very complicated, especially during periods of changes in growth trends. Then, we know the difficulty that represents this calculation even for countries such as the USA; therefore, the problem is even worse in markets of emerging economies where productivity and population growth are much greater.

Once the rationality of private agents is accepted, it is necessary to consider that there are factors that are not included in the rules, such as liquidity crisis in the financial markets, which oblige the European System of Central Banks to modify the rate of interest, i.e., force central bankers to engage in discretionary policy.[19]

In addition, expectations influence the transition between policy rules when a rule is in operation for a long time. Therefore, people adjust their expectations with the policy in operation; however, in the immediate aftermath of the new rule, the agents do not understand the new policy or have to believe in it and therefore, are uncertain if that rule will remain in the medium and/or long term.

Then, because the expectations "only" gradually converge during the transition period, assuming rational expectations, "the impact of this rule on the economy will be different than anticipated" (Taylor, 1993). In addition, during the transition, there are "natural" rigidities in the economy that make it even more difficult to obtain results by a new rule, from activities such as projects, plans, or contracts that the agents have agreed under the terms of the previous policy.[20]

Other objections referred to are as follows:

---

[19]However, the discretionary actions are evaluated around the rule of reference policy.

[20]These rigidities mean that the transition to the new policy must be gradual and announced publicly.

i) The rigid monetary rules specify the authorities' actions, therefore prevent response to unexpected situations (rule proposed by Friedman).

ii) Better results would be obtained if forecasts of inflation and the product, instead of current data, could be incorporated into rule.

The various developments in the field of policy rules include the headlines by different authors, such as Bernanke, Krugman, and Yellen.[21] This includes their rules proposals that are innovative and somehow misinformed; sometimes there have also been misinterpretations regarding some suggested monetary policy rules. Therefore, the fundamental characteristics of these developments have led to these authors engaging in structural errors. Such errors will be reviewed below. The arguments of Bernanke and Yellen were both miscalculations of the Taylor policy rule, while Bernanke just took another rule for his calculations by which he got obviously false and wrong conclusions.

The March 1, 2010, a heated discussion between the chairman of the FED, Bernanke and Toomey was held, in which the first ensured that the Taylor rule is a mechanism that leads to an interest rate below 0% and this therefore justifies the quantitative easing. This is very strange, since by definition, the Taylor (1993) rule does not require an interest rate below zero. The current data for September 1, 2010, said that the inflation rate was approximately 1.5% and the output gap was approximately −5% (Taylor, 2001). So earlier data suggest a rate of federal funds of 0.75% and show that Bernanke made a calculation error.

Then, when Toomey questioned whether Bernanke believed that the Taylor rule induced to interest rates below zero, Bernanke did not respond directly but said that what Taylor (2011) had decided was to opt for another type of rule, which described a behavior of the interest rates of federal funds very different from the one published by John Taylor in 1993. Subsequently, the Toomey emphasized that the Taylor rule suggests higher interest rates relative to the current ones, to which the FED chairman argued that there is a wide range of policy rules working effectively, leading to interest rates below zero.

To this, John Taylor responded that the rule of the monetary policy raised in 1999 is not preferred in the place of that suggested in 1993 and says that possibly the document which referred to Bernanke is "a historical analysis of monetary policy rules," which deals with two different policy

[21]Currently serves as Vice President of the Board of Governors of the Federal Reserve System. Previously, he worked in positions of importance in the Federal Reserve Bank of San Francisco.

rules during different periods in the history of the USA. Taylor makes reference to a rule of policy (suggesting) and another that "other" people prefer. By "other" people, he referred to people from the Federal Reserve. Thus, the inclusion of that rule was the result of the motivation of Taylor after a full analysis.

In this regard, Taylor said that he did not propose another rule and was surprised that someone has interpreted it that way. He argues that it is not of subtleties and that it is necessary to correct those who have said that the Taylor rule is one coefficient that is much greater in the output gap; it is for this reason that "those" determined that the 1993 rule leads to lower-than-zero rates. Then, "the discussion between Bernanke and Toomey suggests that the FED is not clear on what interest rate-based monetary policy strategy to follow" (Taylor, 2011), i.e., whether they are based on the rule proposed by Taylor in 1993, that of 1999, or some other rule.[22]

Also, the Vice President of the Federal Reserve, Yellen, in a speech for the markets of money on April 13, 2012, provided a useful description of the way in which she and other monetary policymakers think analytically about monetary policy rules. In this respect, Taylor has argued that the FED has focused very quickly and dramatically to the issue of discretion[23] and if one intends to return to a policy based on rules, it is necessary to analyze the circumstances before acting.

The speech of the Vice President, the FED, indicated that Taylor proposed two different types of rules of monetary policy for the rate of federal funds; the one in 1993 and another based on a document of 1999. However, Taylor does not propose another rule of policy in 1999, which is important to emphasize because those who say the proposal of another rule in 1999 argue that this has a larger coefficient for the output gap and that, therefore, "it would be at risk of generating a rate close to or equal to zero" (Taylor, 2012).

In his speech, Yellen says that simple rules have improved performance in a wide variety of models and tend to be more robust. Since several simple rules in the literature have been raised, it is clear that their policy implications differ completely depending on their specifications (Yellen,

---

[22]Thus, if the FED strategy was guided by the Taylor rule, then what has been termed as the specificity of the rule would follow (Taylor rule). Then, data provided by the same Taylor established that by February 25, 2011, the rate of inflation was 1.4% and that the output gap was 4.4%. This implies an interest rate of federal funds $(1.4)+(0.5)\times(-4.4)+1=2.1+(-2.2)+1=0.9\%$ or ~1% for that period or quarter.

[23]Taylor says that there is strong evidence that the rules-based policy is working, unpredictable policies (discretion) are harmful. There is evidence that Taylor makes reference to the empirical study of Friedman, Schwartz, and Meltzer. See (Taylor, 2012) in The Wall-Street Journal).

2012). Given the statutory nature of the mandate of maximum employment and price stability, the FED is a reasonable (says Yellen) central bank
focusing on two streaks that prescribed that the federal funds rate should
be adjusted in response to two gaps: the deviation of the inflation from
its long-term objective and deviating from its "normal" rate of long-term
unemployment.

The previous argument of the Vice President of the FED assumes two
errors that Taylor obviously noticed. I mean that Yellen believes that Taylor proposed two types of rules, one in 1993 and the other in 1999. However, it is clear that in his speech and the rule description, she assumes
two breaches other than those established by Taylor, those concerning the
economic activity gap, which is represented by unemployment but by a
gap of GDP.

Therefore, her speech is wrong due to a misinterpretation. Therefore,
Professor Taylor responds to the Vice President of the FED, Yellen, by the
following argument: "assuming 2% inflation, the Taylor rule means that
the federal funds rates should locate in 1% even though a negative output gap of 6% is assumed." This means, $1 = (1.5) \times (2) + (.5) \times (-6) + 1$
. Therefore, the implied rate of the Taylor rule is higher even for a difference of <4%. Therefore Taylor rule aims for central role to the central
bank in making decisions concerning the rate of interest in a way that
the least possible change is incurred in discretionary practices and, in this
way, the main goal of price stability is achieved.

Now, it is a fact that there are economists who have changed the coefficients to the Taylor rule, adding more or less weight to inflation or product
gaps. Some others have tried to use numerical projections to the gaps mentioned instead of observed data.[24] The limitations that the Taylor rule has
is in regards to the use of projections, which is probably necessary to incur
methods as extrapolation (Hilsenrath, 2009), which means descending or
ascending inflation, i.e., biased estimates are obtained. An additional argument in favor of the use of forecasts is that they are relevant because the
Taylor rule is based on a *forward-looking* behavior.[25]

A recognized author, Krugman, used in 2009 a predicted version of the
Taylor rule. The Krugman rule was based on a rule estimated by Rude-
busch at the San Francisco FED and is as follows:

---

[24]There are also discussions about what type of inflation data to use (the general index or an underlying
measure that excludes items such as food and energy).
[25]On this point, Taylor shows a stand completely against it, arguing that in fact the rule was formulated
in the sense that you get a better estimate taking into account the present position to then react.

the federal funds rate target $= 2.07 + (1.28) \times (\text{inflation}) - (1.95) \times (\text{excess of unemployment})$.

Here, inflation is the change of the four quarters in the deflator for personal consumption expenditure(PCE, by its acronym in English) and the excess of the unemployment is the difference between the observed unemployment rate and estimation of the nonaccelerating inflation rate of unemployment (by its acronym in English), which then was 4.8% (Krugman, 2009).

Using current data, according to Krugman, the rule says that the federal funds rate should settle at −5.6%, since it is very difficult to sustain a rate lower than zero for bonds. Then, if you think that the Taylor rule was a good guide for monetary policy in the past, the FED not should start to increase rates until the rule prescribes it. Paul Krugman rejected that the rule can assume positive values because unemployment for 2010 was marginally lower than it was in the last quarter of 2009 and because inflation continued to fall, which implies that for all four quarters of 2010, the federal funds rate would be located in approximately −5.5%.[26]

In response to the above, Taylor emphasizes his disagreement of August 24, 2009, regarding the use of the estimated policy rule, arguing that its use results in repeat mistakes of the past. He says that his rule has worked well and there is no reason to modify it. Therefore, Taylor says that some issues of the Taylor rule should be considered: does it help determine when the FED should start to move its target interest rate above zero? Serves as a measure to detect what should be the so-called orthodox FED's actions? And a considerable deviation from the Taylor rule is seen by many as the main cause of the financial crisis in this year?

The principal work of the Taylor Foundation was the search and determination of a line of simple reference for the FED and other central banks. The result was the fixing of interest rate to prevent frequent recessions and high inflation rates as those experienced in the 1970s. Specifically, it raised the possibility that interest rate should react once and half of once to break through the GDP, more average the inflation rate, more is the unit. It was thus that this rule not only became the online guide, it took over the role of central banks, providing an almost exact description for decision making over a long period in which there was good economic performance.

---

[26]Even though unemployment forecasts dropping modest reductions, federal funds would remain below zero, according to Krugman.

Inflation at the end of August 2009 was around 2%, and the output gap was approximately 8% lower than normal (−8%) since the GDP declined strongly during the recession. Therefore, the Taylor rule says that the interest rate should be 1.5 times 2, more 0.5 times −8, +1, i.e., $3 - 4 + 1 = 0$, a value close to that ranked as the target interest rate of the Federal Reserve. This suggests that if the inflation increases or the output gap narrows, then the FED should increase the federal funds rate.

Thus, the problem is that people have started to modify the Taylor rule. For example, people have suggested increasing the ratio of the product of 0.5–1% with good intentions, react more strongly to changes in the output gap, and begin the transition from a hierarchical regime to a dual one. However, the prevailing conditions in the last quarter of 2009 turned out to be a radical change, in which the gap of −8% of GDP certify that the federal funds rates are below the reference, which means, at least 8% less than zero.[27]

There are also other economists who have proposed their own modifications. Those of the group Goldman Sachs Inc. wanted to rectify the words "inflation rate" in rule by "the forecast of the inflation rate." This no doubt would cause a major change in the interest rate target, since if you forecast deflation rather than an inflationary process, then the target for the federal funds rate will be less than zero. This is what would happen if such changes are applied to the Taylor rule, and it should be noted that there is nothing wrong in wanting to change the rules whenever there is a coherent and rational thought. In any case, "times change and we learn lessons of history" (Taylor, 2009a).

Then, Taylor named Robert Hall of Stanford University since he proposed corrections to the Taylor rule in the opposite direction on the basis of considerations of optimal policy. For this reason, Taylor argues that one of the advantages of the rules is that they reduce the arbitrary discretion and inject predictability to monetary policy decisions. The ability to predict private economic agents is the main factor in favor of the rules, but if very frequent rule changes occur or simply arise, instability and uncertainty are generated.

Continuing on developments to the rules of monetary policy, I think that it is necessary to give a look to what Taylor and Williams exposed in 2010, I am referring to the document that reviews the robustness of and

---

[27]If the benchmark interest rate is below zero by 4% points, then inflation can greatly increase and the economy can grow strongly and, therefore, the FED will not raise interest rates for a considerable time.

simplicity of monetary policy rules. This document highlights the contribution raised by Taylor (1999a) and Führer (1997) in which, although they are based on the generalized form of the Taylor rule, they proposed the addition of "inertia" in the behavior of the interest rate. This allows the possibility that "the policy will respond to expected values or the lagging inflation and the output gap" (Taylor and Williams, 2010).

A key aspect of a simple policy rule is the measurement of appropriate inflation included in the rule. The models presented by Levin, Wieland, and Williams (1999, 2003) conclude that "simple rules that respond to mild rates of inflation (annual rate) have better performance than those that respond to a quarterly inflation rate, even if the objective of the policy is to stabilize the quarterly inflation rate" (Taylor and Williams, 2010). Obviously, rules that react to mild or moderate inflation measures prevent strong variations in the interest rate.

Another relevant aspect is the one spoken about by Batini and Haldane (1999); these authors claim that the presence of lags in the transmission mechanism of monetary policy is difficult and that this is understood as a *forward-looking* policy.[28] From the previous context, authors such as Levin, Wieland, and Williams (1999, 2003) "show that rules that respond to forecasts of inflation in the long run (future) are likely to generate indeterminations on models that include the rational expectations hypothesis" (Taylor and Williams, 2010).

KEYWORDS

---

[28]In this regard, the policy inertia can be significant and, thus, helps to improve the character of *forward-looking* models.

- **Economic policy,**
- **Financial crisis,**
- **Price stability,**
- **Policymakers,**
- **Federal Reserve,**
- **GDP**

CHAPTER 4

MEXICO: INFLATION-TARGETING APPROACH 2001–2012

CONTENTS

This approach – when construed as a framework for making monetary policy, rather than as a rigid rule – has a number of advantages, including more transparent and coherent policymaking, increased accountability, and greater attention to long-run considerations in day-to-day policy debates and decisions.

—Ben S. Bernanke and Frederic S. Mishkin, 1997

Inflation-targeting approach (IT) is a tool widely known for its influence on the monetary policy of many countries, particularly in emerging market economies. Therefore, it is evident that this scheme has caused different reactions among central bankers or persons responsible for the implementation of monetary policy. These reactions have been both in favor, detailing its usefulness as a mechanism for the anchoring of expectations, and against, arguing the possibility of admitting discretion in the actions of the issuing institution.

To some central bankers, inflation targeting is an efficient way to professionalize monetary policy actions, i.e., easier decision making. In general terms, an outline of the main objective of monetary policy is to provide to the economy a nominal anchor.[1] In the recent past (several decades), orthodox stabilization plans have tried to anchor the money supply through a monetary target, i.e., through amounts. Also, heterodox stabilization programs have used the type of change as a fundamental tool.[2]

Given the context, to avoid money laundering, inflation anchors the expectations of inflation via the inflation rate. This means that "the targets of inflation do not anchor the price level but anchor the rate of variation of the expected prices" (Ortiz, 2008). Then, inflation targeting can provide to the economy a nominal anchor through an artifact to coordinate expectations toward the desired point, through the provision to the operators deprived of a reference (numerical target or range of variability).

---

[1] A nominal variable is that used by policymakers to implement monetary policy and that can be used to tie the price level. It is generally accepted that a strong and solid nominal anchor helps ensure that the central bank focuses on long-term policies and resists the temptation of discretionary practices (short-term expansionary policies) that are clearly inconsistent with the objective of stability in the long term (Ortiz, 2008).

[2] Both stabilization mechanisms have not been successful. On the one hand, the monetary target presents some problems when acting as a nominal anchor because the relationship between money and inflation is usually unstable. On the other hand, according to Blanching, the exchange rate works as long as there is perfect capital mobility and two important disadvantages are *i)* the linked country is not able to implement its own monetary policy and use it to respond to shocks that are independent of the country of reference, this means, that the country with the exchange rate anchor cannot influence the decisions of monetary policy of the country to the former has anchored nominally and *ii)* under certain conditions, exchange rate-based stabilization leaves the country prone to speculative attacks.

4.1   THE APPROACH OF THE BANCO DE MÉXICO

For the Banco de México (BANXICO), inflation is the increase in sustained and widespread prices of goods and services in an economy over time.[3] Also, it is considered that inflation adversely affects economic development because it alters the functioning of markets and, therefore, interferes with the efficient allocation of resources. A key feature of the BANXICO posture is that it considers excess money to be a determinant of long-term inflation, which means that if the relevant authorities create money beyond the public demand, the growth of the money supply is increased, which leads to an increase in the level of prices and therefore to an increase in inflation.[4]

One more determinant of long-term inflation, for BANXICO, is the fiscal deficit financed with a loan from the central bank. Such deficit arises through the increase in the monetary base (the sum of bank notes, coins, and the only account of the bank's balance), resulting in an increase in the price level. In addition to the above, inconsistent policies are a source of inflationary pressure in the sense that there is the possibility of some apparently correct policies generating certain inertia related to inflation.

Among the determinants of short-term contraction of aggregate supply are the following.[5] When one posts a decrease in supply added due to increased costs associated with the production processes (e.g., the price of oil), companies increase their prices to maintain their profit margins. On the other hand, an increase in aggregate demands[6] for most goods and services that the economy can produce causes an increase in prices, because there is much money for few goods. Also, when the interest rate decreases, people are incentivized to invest and consume, because money in the banks is not the best option, due to which the quantity available in the economy is increased, which causes the price level to increase. In addition, inflation distorts the price mechanism, which induces an inefficient allocation of resources. When high levels of inflation are registered, consumers and businesses do not have enough information on the levels of relative prices.

---

[3]The increase in price of a single good or service is not considered inflation. If all the prices in the economy rise only once, that is not inflation.

[4]In Mexico, the National Index of Consumer Prices (INPC) is the indicator that measures, over time, the average changes in prices of a weighted basket of goods and services representative of the consumption of households across the country.

[5]Aggregate supply is the total volume of goods and services produced by an economy.

[6]Aggregate demand is the volume of goods and services required by an economy.

Therefore, inflation complicates decisions about which products to buy and produce, increasing the uncertainty related to consumption and investment for the future. Inflation also causes an arbitrary redistribution of wealth between creditors and debtors, who agree to a nominal interest rate, i.e., a rate of interest without adjustment for inflation.[7]

The position and the approach of the inflationary phenomenon should focus on the performance of BANXICO to achieve price stability. To do this, it is necessary to refer to the monetary policy of BANXICO, which has shifted toward the IT. The official features of the monetary policy that BANXICO has adopted are listed as follows: *i*) price stability is the primary objective of monetary policy; *ii*) the central bank should be autonomous; this means that it must have the freedom to make the decisions of monetary policy that it considers relevant; and *iii*) medium-term inflation targeting must be made known to the public.

In January 1999, the Government Board of the BANXICO proposed, as a medium-term inflation-targeting step, convergence of the main trading partners of the country by the end of 2003. Since 2002, BANXICO aims to achieve an annual inflation of 3%, which can move within a range of ±1% (measured through the change in INPC). It is important to clarify that the interval around the inflation targeting is not a margin of tolerance. It is only a way to explicitly represent the uncertainty that inevitably surrounds the punctual fulfillment of the goal, because of the volatility to which inflation is subjected and due to the imprecise relationship between monetary policy actions and their results on inflation.

Another element that distinguishes inflation targeting is *iv*) an analysis of all causes of inflation must be to be able to predict its behavior in the future and *v*) should have alternative measures of inflation as "core inflation." Also for the BANXICO, the inflation-targeting scheme, as they call it, offers a series of benefits, which are listed below: *i*) greater transparency and understanding of the public about the application and decision-making process in the field of monetary policy, *ii*) inflation reduction and consolidation of price stability to identify the sources of inflation and act in a timely manner, *iii*) better accountability, and *iv*) stabilization of the expectations of the public on future inflation.

Now, given that the BANXICO may not directly influence the prices of all goods and services in the economy, it identifies economic variables that could influence directly and other variables that may affect economic

---

[7]Because inflation affects the real value of what is received or paid, what determines the net benefit is the real interest rate, i.e., the nominal interest rate minus inflation.

activity and, therefore, which in turn impact inflation. According to the Bank, monetary policy tools are the open market operations and liquidity instruments.[8] In addition, BANXICO notes that variables that can influence directly (operational) are short-term interest rate and the accounts of the banks at the central bank and those variables beyond the control of the central institution (intermediate) are the interest rate on long-term inflation expectations, the monetary aggregates/credit, and exchange rate.

To fulfill its functions, the central bank is the only one that can create or destroy money or the monetary base. In this regard, the central bank is the only institution that can cover the missing or remove the surplus of liquidity. Derived from the above, the central institution can impose a specific balance of bank accounts, i.e., force banks to maintain certain amount of money in cash in their individual accounts. Similarly, it can set the price of money, i.e., the price at which it creates or removes the monetary base. This is equivalent to setting the interest rate. Thus, the variables that the central bank can influence directly are the balances of the current accounts of the banks or the interest rates applicable to unique accounts (target rate).[9] We will review the type of mandate under which BANXICO is governed.

4.1 MANDATE

Price stability is the primary objective of the BANXICO, and this is stipulated in the Constitution and in the own law of the BANXICO. This means that the issuing institution has by law a mandate of unique character, which can be represented by a loss function, which is assigned a value of zero to γ, so effectively, monetary authorities react exclusively to the deviations of the observed inflation (π_i) with respect to the target (π^T), as shown in the following loss function.

---

[8]All banks of the country maintain a deposit account in the BANXICO. In this context, it means liquidity to the sum of the balances of these accounts (also known as bank reserves, unique accounts, or current accounts). If the sum of all unique accounts of the banks is positive, it is said that there is an excess of liquidity (*liquidity surplus*) in the banking system and if the sum is negative, it is said that there is a shortage of liquidity (*liquidity deficit*).

[9]This operational objective will influence inflation in different ways. When BANXICO set a target level for the expected rate, it influences the behavior of long-term interest rates and thus impacts the appropriations granted and the taxes that banks pay to influence, among other variables, economic activity and finally have an impact on inflation.

$$\gamma\left(y_t - y_t^n\right)^2 + (1-\gamma)\left(\pi_t - \pi^T\right)^2 = 0 \qquad (4.1)$$

The above is based primarily, as mentioned above, by the Political Constitution of the Mexican United States in the sixth paragraph of its Article 28, which refers to the monopolistic practice.

> ...The State will have a central bank which will be autonomous in the exercise of its functions and its administration. Its main objective will be to ensure the stability of the purchasing power of the national currency, thereby strengthening the stewardship of national development which corresponds to the State. No authority may order the Bank grant funding.

The above is related to the costs of BANXICO associated with inflation. Obviously, these costs are of a social nature, since inflation reduces the real value of money, i.e., it decreases the amount of goods and services that money can buy, thus affecting the purchasing power of people on fixed incomes and discourages saving. In this regard, it is convenient in every way to emphasize the posture and scopes of the Mexican Central Bank; this is cited in the law of the BANXICO in its first article, which validates the Constitution

> ...The central bank will be person governed by public law on an autonomous basis and will be called Banco de México. In the exercise of its functions and its administration are governed by the provisions of this law, regulatory of the sixth and seventh paragraphs of article 28 of the political Constitution of the Mexican United States.

To strengthen the above, we move forward to the second and third articles respectively

> ...The Banco de México will have purpose provide the economy of the country's national currency. The achievement of this purpose you will have as a priority to ensure the stability of the purchasing power of the currency. Promote the healthy development of the financial system and promote the proper functioning of the payment systems shall also be objectives of the Bank."

Here, it stands out that the central bank aims to promote the financial system and the payment system to play in the most efficient manner possible. I also think it convenient to deal with the relation of the third article to the law to highlight the main functions of the BANXICO.

> ...The Bank shall perform the following functions:
>
> I.   Regulating the issuance and circulation of currency, changes, the brokerage and financial services, as well as payment systems;

II. Operate with credit institutions as bank reserve and sending of last resort;

III. Providing treasury services to the Federal Government and to act as financial agent of the same;

IV. Serve as Advisor to the Federal Government in matters economic and, particularly, financial.

Once we have spoken concerning the mandate of the BANXICO, we should now refer to the way in which the issuing institution operates such a mandate, this means the mechanisms of transmission of the Mexican Central Bank need to be immediately explained.

4.2 TRANSMISSION MECHANISMS

When a bank needs cash resources, it has two options: borrow the money from another bank or ask for money from the central bank. If the rate charged by any of the two optional institutions is the same, it should be indifferent from whom the bank borrows the money. The rate at which the banks lend together is known as the rate of bank funding and fulfills the same role as the interest rate at which the Central Bank lends. BANXICO aims to operationalize the "rate of bank funding to one day" from January 2008.

Interest rate movements will affect inflation in different ways. The above are referred to formally as channels of monetary policy transmission. The stance of monetary policy is unveiled through the announcement of changes in the rate of bank funding to within 1 day: an increase in this rate indicates a more restrictive monetary policy stance and a decrease indicates a more relaxed posture. The monetary policy stance is that if inflation goes up, then the central bank must raise the rate of funding, making monetary policy more restrictive. On the contrary, if the inflation is low, the rate of funding would have to be reduced.

When the BANXICO makes mention of transmission mechanisms, it usually refers to the transmission of the families' saving channel. An increase in the rate of bank funding for a day causes a spike in long-term interest rates, encourages saving for better yields, and reduces the consumption by families. On the contrary, if the rate of bank funding is lowered to a day, saving becomes less attractive and families may prefer to consume more. Another channel of transmission is via credit. An increase in the target banking rate makes the realization of new investment projects less attractive due to the higher costs involved.

On the other hand, if target rate is low, investment projects become more attractive.

A third channel of transmission for the central bank is the exchange rate.[10] With flexible exchange rate, a rise in interest rates can lead to an entry of foreign investors due to better yields, causing the Mexican "peso" worth more.[11] This change in the exchange rate causes the foreign goods to become cheaper in comparison with the national goods, diminishing the demand for national goods and, therefore, their prices.[12]

It is important to clarify that the unique mandate of BANXICO is in line with the set of transmission mechanisms affecting other key variables, specifically the inflation, for the good performance of a central institution that operates under the IT. In addition, it should be noted that the first four channels of transmission, viz., i) interest rates, ii) credit, iii) prices of other assets, and iv) the exchange rate, which the BANXICO referred to are directly influenced by the short-term interest rate, while the expectations channel is served or affected from the actions of the issuing institution even more directly (see Figure 4.1).

To achieve an integral communication strategy responsible for this task, the groups that will be directed and the pathways and communication tools are defined to be used. In this regard, many central banks have been taking schemes of targets of inflation as a monetary policy framework. Under this scheme, since the central bank undertakes to defend and fulfill quantitative inflation targeting, the need for an open and constant communication has become much more stringent. For all of the above, it is necessary to promptly review the process by which Mexico adopted the IT.

---

[10]There is also the expectations channel. This channel refers to the effects of decisions of the BANXICO on what people expect to happen with prices and economic growth.

[11]That is, an appreciation of the local currency is carried out. The single exchange rate rises or lowers, which results in appreciated or depreciated currencies, respectively.

[12]Additionally, for companies that have debt denominated in foreign currency or have raw materials imported, the lowering of the dollar (or any other foreign currency) can reduce costs if they opt to buy abroad; the demand for domestic goods then falls and, therefore, inflation reduces.

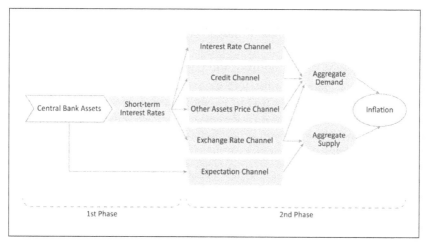

(From Banco de México. With permission.)

FIGURE 4.1   Transmission Mechanism of Monetary Policy.

A key aspect of inflation targeting regarding another type of monetary policy is the public announcement of a numerical target. This is the nominal anchor that serves as reference for inflation expectations. It is for this reason that the former Governor of the BANXICO, Ortiz (2012) considers that the implementation of monetary policy through a scheme of inflation targeting is a game repeated between the authorities and economic operators in the context of asymmetric information. In addition, transparency and accountability functions are aimed at improving the interdependent relationship between agents. Thus, private actors are well informed about the allocation of resources.

In addition, better communication between the monetary authority and private economic agents leads to a lower dispersion of expectations, reducing the variance in relative prices, which leads to the reduction of the levels of inflation (Ortiz, 2012). Therefore, the reduction of this dispersion may improve the transmission mechanism of monetary policy and, therefore, the expectations. For Guillermo Ortiz, the Head of the Mexican Issuing Institution (1998–2010), the characteristics that should cover the management of the IT were essentially three: *i*) the central bank is committed to a single numeric target (either level or range) for annual inflation; *ii*) inflation forecast is an intermediate target; and *iii*) it plays a decisive role in terms of transparency, accountability, and communication with the public.

The definition of the target of inflation can be *i*) a timely target, *ii*) a target range, or *iii*) a tolerance range. This type of blank determinations provide flexibility to the central banker to conduct monetary policy, as well as allowing deviations from the target to face temporary *shocks* to avoid frequent changes in the interest rate. Regarding the forecast of inflation, according to BANXICO, it is well known that "monetary policy is most effective if it is guided by forecasts, because there is a lag between the actions of monetary policy and its impact on the target variables of central banks" (Ortiz, 2008).

The latter represents a noticeable variation from what the Taylor *tripod* prescribed; this means, expected inflation is replaced by a predicted inflation. Guillermo Ortiz emphasized their position, citing Svensson (1997), when he noted that "targets of predicted inflation" involve defining the instrument rate (trend), which approximates to their target in a specific time horizon.

From the point of view of the Mexican Central Bank, the IT provides three benefits: *i*) this scheme successfully reduced inflation and makes it less volatile; *ii*) it reduces the costs of disinflation; and *iii*) it anchors the expectations of long-term inflation targeting. It is also necessary to meet certain requirements, such as a fiscal policy favorable to low inflation (reduced fiscal deficits), the autonomy of the central bank, and the opening of the economy to international trade.

Some of the benefits in emerging countries given this outline of monetary policy are, according to the former Governor of the BANXICO that the level and volatility of inflation are reduced considerably more significant reductions in average inflation and variability of the product are experienced, the dispersion of long-term inflation expectations are lower, and the nominal system of the economy as well as the institutional structure of monetary policy are improved. In this way, in general terms, the conditions under which Mexico joined the group of countries that make use of the IT as a structure of reference for the management of monetary policy are outlined below.

4.3 MACROECONOMIC BALANCE ENTERING INFLATION TARGETING

This section consists of a review of the macroeconomic characteristics of Mexico before the adoption of the IT as the fundamental axis of the economy and, therefore, the monetary stance of the issuing institution, i.e., the BANXICO. In the analysis of the aggregate balance, the behavior of variables such as the exchange rate, international reserve levels, public debt, the level of prices, etc. will be reviewed even before the inclusion of inflation targeting by Mexico officially in 2001.

Figure 4.2 shows the performance of the variables "exchange rate" and "international reserves" for the period 1997–2011. Here, the exchange rate was flexible, and international reserves registered a very significant upward trend since the beginning of the period under analysis. The above contributed and continues to do so to the stability of the exchange rate variable, except for the years 2008 and 2009, in which the international level of reserves dropped (due to the effects of the *subprime* crisis in 2007) to avoid major negative implications arising from the increase in the variation of the exchange rate.

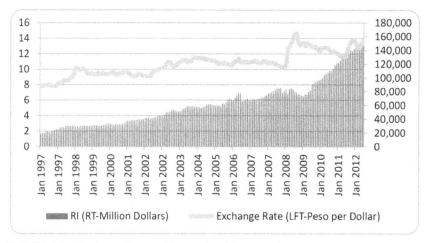

FIGURE 4.2   Exchange Rate and International Reserves in Mexico, 1997–2011.

(Own elaboration with data from the Banco de México and the Center for Studies of Public Finance [CEFP]. With permission.)

Moreover, Figure 4.3 shows the behavior of total net debt for the period from 1995 to 2011. It is necessary to note here that Mexico was prepared since the mid-1990s to adequately take up the IT, therefore revealing a very stable performance (slight upward trend) of debt of 1995 in mid-2008. This period of relative stability of debt was interrupted by additional public sector financing requirements arising from the financial crisis that took place in the mortgage industry in the USA.

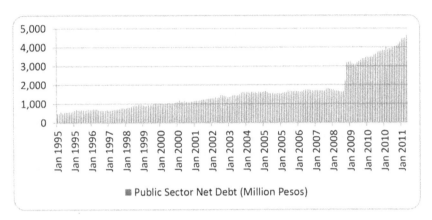

FIGURE 4.3   Total Net Debt of the Public Sector in Mexico, 1995–2011.[a]
[a]Balances at the end of the period.
(Compiled with data obtained from the Banco de México. With permission.)

We continue with the relationship between gross domestic product (GDP) and the level of prices, which is parsed from 1994 until 2011, see Figure 4.4. It is clear that the relationship between these two variables (a real one and the other nominal) is reverse and this association is clear in the year 1995, the year in which there was a crisis, accompanied by a major devaluation of the Mexican peso against the US dollar. However, in 2003 and 2007, economic and financial crises were also raised and there was the same behavior as with the crisis of 1994–1995. This was due to that in the first period, the country still had not adopted the IT, while in the subsequent two periods, the country was immersed in the monetary policy scheme.

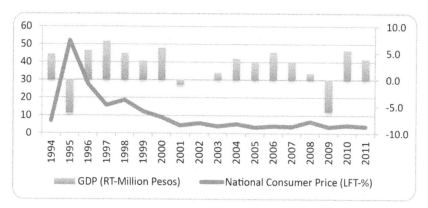

FIGURE 4.4   Gross Domestic Product[a] and National Consumer Price[b] in Mexico, 1994–2011.

[a]and [b]represent annual rates of variation.

(Homemade with CEFP data. With permission.)

The following Figure 4.5 refers to the net credit, whose definition by the central bank refers to the placement of their monetary investment in international assets, liabilities, or to grant credit to residents. This concept was used for the first time in 1977 due to the fact that previously, "the position of residents was not consolidated in a single concept" (war of Moon and Sanchez, 2004). In this way, on the one hand, international reserve is now considered the net position of the central bank abroad. On the other hand, the NET internal credit is considered the position with residents and the monetary liabilities comprise the position on banknotes and coins.[13]

In this way, the monetary base intends to attach with the net domestic credit; this relationship registers a divergent behavior since 1995 (the year in which they were practically the same) until 2012, at which point its position is completely opposite. Thus, while it increases the monetary base, net credit is restricted, which means that the central bank increasingly has limited funding for the Government and commercial banks with the stabilization premise.

---

[13]This approach has the disadvantage that it does not register the entire monetary base. It should also be noted that the concept of banknotes and coins is determined by factors other than the Bank reserves and mostly is in the hands of the residents of the nonbanking private sector, i.e., the position of the central bank with the resident private sector is to be considered.

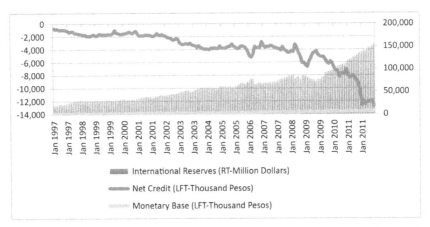

FIGURE 4.5   Net Credit,[a] Monetary Base,[b] and International Reserves in Mexico, 1997–2012.

[a]Nominal balances and [b]sources and uses of the monetary base, applications, notes, and coins in circulation among the public.

(Homemade with BANXICO data. With permission.)

At the same time, it is convenient to record the performance of interest rates to determine, to some extent, the structure of interest rates. Figure 4.6 shows the close relationship between interbank equilibrium interest rates used by the Mexican issuing institution for signaling the stance of the monetary policy to the commercial banks. However, as of 2008, the BANXICO published the target rate as the explicit reference of monetary policy, i.e., the operations of the central bank were carried out through its policy instrument, converging the market rate of the target.

Before the publication of the target rate, the Mexican Central Bank operated through an "auxiliary" rate to determine its stance of monetary policy; this means that it implicitly used a target for the interest rate that was consistent with the inflation target of 3%±1% of variability.

Once the economic context in which the country was before the IT is established generally, the second part of this chapter aims to establish major deviations in the use of inflation targeting from the standard. In addition, there are implications of such variations in the implementation of the scheme on monetary policy.

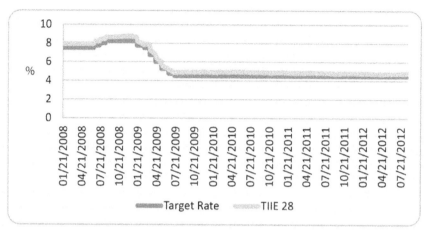

FIGURE 4.6   Interest Rates in Mexico, 2000–2011.
(Homemade with Banco de México data. With permission.)

4.2   DEVIATIONS FROM THE STANDARD APPROACH

The effects of global integration, such as increased international trade in goods and services, recovery of global financial flows, and some of the benefits associated with such integration, such as "improved well-being and growth due to a better allocation of resources, greater specialization in production, and the transfer of technology by foreign direct investment flows," have forced countries to implement more orthodox macroeconomic schemes. The options, according to Ortiz (2000), are as follows:

i)   The creation of monetary unions, boxes of conversion, or the uni- lateral adoption of a foreign currency.

ii) Application of more flexibility in the exchange rate and greater independence in monetary policy.

However, without coordination and a certain degree of flexibility, the main approach involves a difficult process of adjustment in response to real shocks, generating a necessary level of deflation that will accommodate the changes in the real exchange rate. Therefore, the difficulty of coordination, especially between emerging and developed countries, as well as the limited economic flexibility exhibited by most of the countries leaves the regime of flexible exchange rate as the most attractive alternative for developed countries with open capital accounts.[14]

Ortiz said that the balance of payments and the 1994–1995 financial crisis forced Mexico to adopt a flexible exchange rate. It was thought that, at that time, the conditions were not favorable for the adoption of the flexible exchange rate regime in the medium term. Once the macroeconomic situation in the country recovered, in terms of Mexico's debt and financial issues, its access to capital markets improved. It was only then that the BANXICO was able to accumulate international reserves and decrease the volatility of financial variables.[15]

Among the benefits of adopting a floating exchange rate is allowing response to *shocks*, since it discourages the entry of short-term capital flows. Referring to the benefits, Ortiz argued that it also allows adjustments to the level of the nominal exchange rate in response to internal and external *shocks* that affect the level of the real exchange rate. It also restricts the output volatility and allows the central bank to follow an independent monetary policy. "As a result, the performance of Mexico in terms of growth and employment during the period 1998–2000 was better than most of the countries of the region" (Ortiz, 2000).

With respect to the costs associated with a flexible exchange rate, it can be mentioned that all investors must bear a risk premium automatically due to greater volatility, increasing domestic interest rates. Another aspect to be highlighted is that the information contained in the exchange rate is limited if the market is small and controlled by a small number of agents. Finally, absence or low level of development of the derivatives market allows coverage of foreign exchange risks, which implies higher costs in the form of an efficient allocation of the resources of actors such as banks, businesses, and individuals.[16]

The former Governor of the BANXICO defends the flexible exchange rate stance, arguing that some emerging countries have recorded a significant financial vulnerability because they are the countries that recently adopted this exchange system, after a balance of payments crisis. Yet, Ortiz, proposes three fundamental lines to reduce the risks associated with

---

[14]From 1990 to 1999, the number of countries with this exchange rate regime went up from 16.2% to 27.6% (Ortiz, 2000).

[15]At the same time, a strong development of the derivatives market, associated with the peso/dollar exchange rate, was what enabled the players to hedge exchange-rate volatility.

[16]These effects include financial fragility of the country and lack of liquidity. Financial vulnerability leads to greater exchange rate volatility.

financial fragility: *i*) development of the derivatives market, *ii*) policy on debt management and liquidity management, and *iii*) development of long-term domestic debt market, whether through the setting of nominal rates or through indexing of bonds to the national price index for the country in question.

The development of the capital market allows domestic agents to cover themselves against exchange rate movements. Once flexible exchange rate is adopted, businesses and industries internalize the risks involved with the currency borrowing. Therefore, "the Mexican experience has shown that the adoption of flexible exchange rate will help limit the currency exposure of the Mexican companies" (Ortiz, 2000). The public sector acted similarly by the adequacy of debt and liquidity management policies. Thus, the Government increased the maturity and limited the concentration of foreign debt.

With regard to the implementation of monetary policy in a context of exchange rate flexibility and global integration, in terms of policy formulation, the monetary authority must focus more on the international development of financial and commodity markets and on the performance of those economies with which the country has important actual links. In addition, it is appropriate to revise the odds that in another emerging market, a financial crisis happens due to the potential contagion. This contagion can be even when countries do not submit real links.[17]

From the point of view of Ortiz (2000), global integration, a high level of uncertainty, and limited credibility have considerable effects on the transmission mechanisms. What happens is that the probability that the direct effect on the aggregate demand of changes in interest rates[18] becomes less relevant, while the exchange rate channel takes up importance.[19]

The Mexican case is useful to illustrate what has been explained in the preceding paragraphs. The ratio of trade to GDP increased from 31% to 59% in 10 years (from 1990 to 1999). In addition, there had been a

---

[17]In emerging and open markets, greater financial integration implies that central banks must react quickly and appropriately to new events because of the speed with which credibility is impaired, which means a limited margin of error.

[18]Financial integration allows firms access to external resources of financing. At the same time, greater uncertainty could limit the development of the domestic financial sector due to the risk associated with the loans denominated in domestic currency.

[19]The transmission of the exchange rate channel takes strength due to the fact that by integrating international trade, fundamentals like production, demand, and price variations in exchange-level characteristics become more sensitive.

process of high inflation and episodes of extremeness in the exchange rate changes, resulting in the loss of inflation targeting and, therefore, private economic agents used variations in the exchange rate as reference to the inflation rate, that is, inflation expectations were tied to the behavior of the exchange rate.[20]

In addition, there is a significant *trade-off* for emerging markets between restrictive monetary policies and the vulnerability of the current account. Ortiz (2000) says that to improve such *trade-off*, it is necessary and indispensable to have good fiscal and monetary policy coordination. The situation then prevailing in Mexico perfectly exemplifies the above. During the first half of 2000, the aggregate demand and GDP had grown at annual rates above 10% and 7%, respectively (Ortiz, 2000). Because of the threat that accounted for this growth above the potential for long-term inflation targeting, the BANXICO restricted its policy throughout the year.

This led to rise in real interest rates, which in turn, led to appreciation of the local currency. Mexico experienced a gradual convergence toward the IT. The devaluation and the financial crisis of 1994–1995 gave a brief experience with monetary targets since it was imperative to possess an intermediate target. When inflation fell and the volatility of short-term relationship between monetary growth and inflation became evident, the central bank turned toward the emphasis of their target of annual inflation.

It was for this reason that since 1997–1998, the focus of monetary policy in Mexico has been on the process of convergence toward the IT. The main elements of this scheme were as follows (Ortiz, 2000): *i*) a goal of medium-term reduction in inflation, which was paired with the prevailing levels of major trading partners of Mexico for 2003, *ii*) annual inflation targeting, *iii*) a constant assessment of inflationary pressures to guide monetary policy and actions, and *iv*) a policy of full transparency in which quarterly publications on inflation play a key role.

The biggest difference encountered by Ortiz (2000) with respect to the monetary policy scheme in Mexico and that in other countries was that the focus of inflation targeting was the monetary policy instrument used. While other countries used the *medium term* as an instrument of interest rate policy, the BANXICO used a borrowed operational reserve procedure (borrowed book operating procedure). Thus, when the BANXICO requires

---

[20]These factors, according to Ortiz (2000), explained the quick and significant effect (*pass-through*) of transfer movements of the exchange rate variations in the INPC.

to restrict its monetary policy, it should raise its target of borrowed reserves (short).[21]

The damage caused by the crisis forced Mexico to direct its efforts to the stabilization of the economy to ensure that fiscal dominance is not present. Then, it raised three goals; *i*) the Government should fulfill all its obligations; *ii*) economy should be adjusted quickly to a new macroeconomic environment. The current account deficit dropped from 7.1% of GDP in 1994 to 0.61% in 1996 (Ortiz, 2008); and *iii*) a meltdown of the financial system should be prevented.

Those in charge of monetary policy in Mexico had, as a challenge, set monetary policy as the nominal anchor of the economy at the time when there was a great uncertainty about the commitment and of banks' capacity to achieve financial and price stability. The strategy mainly consisted of three elements. The first was to improve transparency in the implementation of monetary policy, the second was to maintain a clear restrictive bias that you induce a sustainable reduction of inflation, and the third element was to respond appropriately to inflationary *shocks*.

During the process by which Mexico traveled to the IT, inflation of about 52% in 1995 fell to levels close to 3% in recent years in the context of flexible exchange (Ortiz, 2008). Thus, for the BANXICO, it was a priority to get transparency, accountability, and reputation. In 1995, it defined a target for the accumulated balance of the current accounts of commercial banks with the central bank (short) as the main instrument for affecting interest rates.

Subsequently, in 1998, to continue with the improvement of the transparency and the effectiveness of monetary policy, announcements of changes in the instruments began to be made public; including discussions of the reasons of why these would change. Then, in 1999, the Mexican Central Bank adopted a medium-term inflation objective for the consumer price index, whose basic motivation was to achieve convergence to inflation levels similar to those of the main trading partners.

A year later, the issuing institution began publishing quarterly inflation reports, which contained detailed discussions of sources of inflationary pressures in its structure and added the concept of core inflation as a determinant for the analysis of inflation, in particular, to assess inflationary *shocks*. Subsequently, the process to improve transparency was reinforced in 2001 since

---

[21]The main motivation in the choice of this instrument, in the Mexican case, was that the frequency of internal and external *shocks*, in conjunction with the rapid effect of exchange on prices, requires frequent and large movements in interest rates.

it was in this year that Mexico formally adopted the IT. For 2003, a target for long-term inflation of 3% was defined, with a variability range.

Given the above, "since 2003, monetary policy announcements have been made on pre-established dates" (Ortiz, 2008). Finally, in 2008, the Mexican Central Bank ceased to use the mechanism of the "short" and monetary policy went on to be orchestrated through an operational target defined by the interbank interest rate overnight. Once the transaction to inflation targeting was more advanced, the target and the implementation of monetary policy was made open to public scrutiny and, therefore, more transparent. This process helped accountability for the most professional BANXICO and to anchor inflation expectations.

Considering that Mexico is an emerging market economy that has been able to reduce inflation under a flexible exchange rate regime, its experience therefore, suggests that when there is no fiscal dominance, the IT is useful to impose discipline on monetary policy and, as a result, provides a nominal anchor to the economy. In addition, says Ortiz, when inflation fell and macroeconomic stability was achieved, the functioning of the rating system was improved.

The former Governor of the BANXICO is convinced that since December 1995, inflation has reduced from 52% to a level that is around 9% in December 2000. At the same time, the IT succeeded in establishing a long-run inflation objective. Also, the BANXICO reacted increasingly to the expectations of the market, a key feature for inflation targeting since this monetary policy scheme as the nominal anchor of the economy has precisely led to inflation expectations. This was accompanied by a significant increase of transparency in the decisions of the central institution, thus reducing the transfer of effect of exchange rate depreciation onto prices.

The International Monetary Fund places Mexico in the group of countries with independent floating, i.e., in a flexible exchange rate regime. However, in some cases, the exchange rate policy actions do not validate the position officially declared. For this reason, this part of the text will evaluate the real position of Mexico, and therefore, some measurements taken in exchange rate terms by monetary and fiscal authorities during the period of study (2000–2011) will be reviewed.

In addition, the validity of the Calvo–Reinhart hypothesis shall be verified. A further deviation that is referred to here is that of the hypothesis raised by Calvo and Reinhart (2002), whereby countries that "say" that they have adopted a flexible exchange rate regime will not apply it strictly.

This means that developing countries, mainly and within Mexico, do not operate their monetary policy through a Taylor *tripod* standard. This is evident in the angle corresponding to the type of exchange rate regime (flexible). Here, Calvo and Reinhart argue that these countries are characterized by what they call "fear of floating."[22]

Developing economies can register high rates of inflation, so there can be a high association between exchange rate and inflation. Therefore, the central bankers fear completely loosening of the country's exchange rate. The BANXICO does not define it as fear of floating, but fear of inflation. However, following the Mexican case, during periods of low inflation, the issuing institution intervenes in the foreign exchange market to limit volatility. In this way, the position of the BANXICO is not setting a certain currency, but intervening to reduce variability (see Figure 4.7).

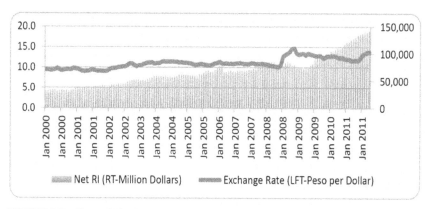

FIGURE 4.7   Fear of Floating (Exchange Rate and International Reserves [RI] in Mexico, 2000–2011).

(Compiled with data from Banco de México and the CEFP, 2012. With permission.)

Then, the options that the Mexican Central Bank has at its disposal are a combination of strategies:

i)   Establish a level of parity, where $e^T = e^0 \cdot y$.
ii) Reduce volatility or variance of the exchange rate (σ_e) to zero or to a range of ±2% approximately. This means that BANXICO has a variability band of 4%, i.e., a moving target, as shown in Figure 4.8.

---

[22]The trend toward exchange rate flexibility had as its main motivation the possibility of addressing external *shocks* through the application of its own monetary policy.

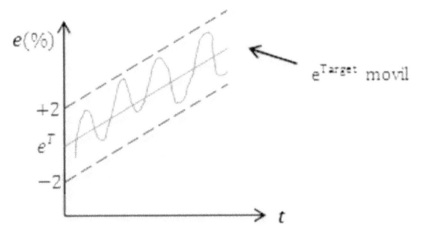

FIGURE 4.8   Fear of Floating.

(Own elaboration based on the Seminar on Macroeconomic Credibility, 2012. With permission.)

According to the methodology of Calvo and Reinhart (2002), which is essentially based on the analysis of the frequency distributions of the monthly variations of the nominal exchange rate, international reserves, and interest rate, we can see that Mexico has seen "fear of floating" when it determined a flexible exchange rate as its official stance. This methodology consists of absolute values of variations and calculates the odd that these were placed within a given range.

Calvo and Reinhart said that the criteria are based on the probability that the monthly variation of the variable is in a given range:

i)   For the fixed exchange rate[23]: the probability that the monthly exchange rate variation is greater with a fixed exchange rate policy and less when rate is flexible.

ii) For international reserves: the probability that the monthly variation is placed within a reference range is less with fixed exchange rate and more with a flexible exchange rate regime. This is so because the reserves are used to prevent depreciations or devaluations of the currency, as the case may be.

iii) For the interest rate: If the monthly variation is very high, then there are problems of credibility, so the probability that the month-

---

[23]The case of the fixed exchange rate is thus due to the greater intervention by fiscal and monetary authorities to maintain the value of the currency.

ly variation is within the range is very low when the authorities do not have credibility in relation to private economic agents.

Table 4.1 shows the results that were derived by Calvo and Reinhart (2002), Reinhart (2000), and Zarate (2010) for two periods in the recent history of Mexico. These periods correspond to managed exchange (dirty water) and flexible (floating) exchange rate. Considering the above, this paper aims to do an additional calculation, for the period from 2007 to 2011. This period was thus established to capture the situation before, during, and after the *subprime* crisis started in the USA. Reference ranges used by the authors mentioned above are ±1% and ±2% for the exchange rate and international reserves, respectively, while for the interest rate, the basis is 400–500 points (4%–5%).

The conclusions reached by Calvo and Reinhart were that Mexico recorded some traits that showed that there was presence of fear to float because the odds of variation associated with exchange rate, interest rate, and international reserves were relatively high and growing between periods with floating exchange rate. The last analysis period is also a calculation of this research. What can be evaluated in this regard is that behavior, in general terms, with respect to prior periods is like the chances of the three variables of study being of high variation; therefore, they complete the review arguing that before, during, and after the *subprime* crisis with its epicenter in the USA, Mexico exhibited a behavior that allows us to say that fear of floating was present.

After the Asian financial crisis and the subsequent crises in Russia, Brazil, and Turkey, the use of the intermediate exchange rate regimes has dissipated and governments have opted for "corner solutions," as they call them (Calvo and Reinhart, 2002). These solutions relate to extreme cases, i.e., fixations of strong currency boards, dollarization, and currency on the one hand; unions and a free floating exchange rate regime on the other: for instance, the abandonment of their national currencies by 20 European countries (euro), while, on the other hand, Ecuador and El Salvador adopted the US dollar as the official currency. By contrast, countries such as South Korea, Thailand, Brazil, Russia, Chile, Colombia, Poland, and Turkey announced their intention to float their currencies (Calvo and Reinhart, 2002).

TABLE 4.1 [24] Fear of Floating in Mexico, 1989–2011

Exchange Rate and Period	Exchange Rate		International Reserves		Interest Rate	
The Reference Value Band	±1%	±2.5%	±1%	±2.5%	±4%	±5%
Managed exchange rate, 1989–1994	64.3	95.7	15.3	31.9	13.9	8.3
Floating exchange rate, 2001–2009[a]	45.7	77.1	31.4	63.8	46.7	41.0
Floating exchange rate, 2007–2011[b]	29.4	57.1	8.7	45.8	61.0	63.5

[a]The estimates for the period 2001–2009 were taken from Zarate (2010).

[b]The calculations for the 2007–2011 period are homemade.

Source: Calvo, G.; Reinhart, C., Fear of floating. Q. J. Econ. 2002, 117(2), 379–408; Reinhart, C., The mirage of floating exchange rates. Am. Econ. Rev. 2000, 90, 2; with data from the Banco de Mexico. With permission

The Calvo–Reinhart hypothesis is based on a study that includes 39 countries and spans the period from January 1970 to November 1999. In this study are countries located in Africa, Asia, Europe, and America, within which Mexico is present, and 155 exchange rate regimes are analyzed. Data from these countries relating to exchange rate, international reserves, and the money market interest rates are reviewed. "Interest rates are included in this analysis because several countries, particularly in recent years, routinely use a policy of interest rates to soften the fluctuations of the exchange rate" (Calvo and Reinhart, 2002).

The strategy of this methodology is to compare "what countries say and which ones meet." What countries say is reported to the International Monetary Fund and are classified into four types of exchange rate regimes:

---

[24]For the production of Table 4.1, it was necessary to determine a critical value for the variability of the rate of exchange, international reserves, and the interest rate. Then, the probability that the monthly change of each variable fell within this critical value was calculated considering different exchange rate regimes.

fixed, limited flexibility, managed floating, and free floating.[25] According to Calvo and Reinhart (2002), interest rates can fluctuate considerably if the monetary authorities actively use rate of interest as a mechanism to stabilize the exchange rate. However, interest rates are intended to be volatile if variations in the exchange rate or inflation expectations are anchored. This is the particular case of authorities that lack or have little credibility.

Involved in the measurement of volatility are the variable exchange rate, international reserves, and nominal interest rates. Under a floating exchange rate of 5%, the conclusion is reached that those countries that enjoy some degree of credibility present a very low probability that the variability of the interest rate exceeds ±4%, accompanied by moderate and high probability that the type change and reserves vary within a range of ±2%, respectively. The above suggests and provides evidence that the authorities of a country in which their actions are not supported or accompanied by acceptance and validation of private economic agents feel the need to incur variations in their interest rates and reservations for a part and intervene in the exchange rate on the other.

There are differences between entities with flexible regimens. These differences relate to the degree of flexibility or the way in which they carry out flotation and are even more apparent in emerging economies, since in such countries, international reserves are used to reduce the volatility of the exchange rate and the interest rate to stabilize the exchange rate variable. Thus, the emerging economies (into which one can classify Mexico) have larger reserves than the developed countries. This behavior has characterized the majority of the Latin American economies that have eased their exchange rate after a currency crisis.[26] Thus, the level of foreign exchange reserves serves as evidence that those countries that have announced full flotation do not really act as they have previously stated (Zárate, 2010).

Now, when it comes to a managed floating regime, countries like Mexico generated greater credibility and, therefore, a lower volatility in interest rate was required. When the behavior of international reserves is analyzed, it is pertinent to note that the variance of international reserves on a free floating

---

[25]It should be noted that bilateral exchange rates are made against the German mark in the case of European countries and the US dollar in other countries.
[26]Latin American countries are most involved in the exchange market, while developed countries are those that are closer to a system of pure exchange rate flexibility.

rate should be zero.[27] However, Calvo and Reinhart (2002) propose factors that influence changes in reserves as follows: *i*) hidden transactions of international reserves where credit lines could be used to defend the exchange rate during periods of speculative pressures, *ii*) in the absence of hidden transactions, countries rely heavily on domestic open market operations and changes in the interest rate to limit variations in the exchange rate.

There is evidence that the authorities are tempted to stabilize the exchange rate through mechanisms in both the international foreign exchange market and open market operations. In addition, "fear of floating" showed that when combined with lack of credibility, a high transfer effect of the exchange rate to prices and the inflation-targeting scheme ensues. However, the union of the IT and emerging flexible exchange rate arises as the most popular alternative to fixed exchange rate. Calvo and Reinhart (2002) propose that discretionary monetary policy serves to exploit the trade-off described by a short-term Phillips curve and has little relevance for emerging countries since a history of high and variable inflation has eliminated any negative exchange between unemployment and inflation surprises. In fact, in many emerging countries, there is a tendency to use inflationary surprises to improve the fiscal position of the Government.

According to Calvo and Reinhart (2002), the reasons why countries exhibit fear behavior toward floating rates are diverse, including the fact that in emerging economies, when strong currency depreciation occurs, the consequences associated with this process cannot be expected, which means that an increase in exports, investment, and the product does not happen. The above does not occur since the country may have a substantial debt in foreign currency, lack of access to international markets, and, from my point of view, the most important factor is that the institutions responsible for these policies lack or have no reputation and credibility that allows validation of their actions.

When there is a high degree of integration among countries, although the value of one currency is not fixed with respect to the other, the decisions of the neighboring country (with better-positioned coin) affect domestic politics, which means that there is no full independence in monetary policy for a country with weak currency. Another factor that influences institu-

---

[27]In the Mexican case, Calvo and Reinhart (2002), only recorded 28% probability that changes in international reserve levels were less than 2.5%. However, there are countries, such as Bolivia, where this probability is even lower.

tions not having an effective and independent monetary policy is the low credibility of institutions, both monetary and fiscal. A way of correcting these problems is the introduction of a scheme of monetary policy based on a rule. Under a flexible parity, it is possible to adopt any monetary policy scheme, which can even be incurred on a discretionary behavior.

However, in the monetary framework, the main consequence of the adoption of a floating exchange rate regime is the loss of the nominal anchor provided by the fixed exchange rate. The solution to this is to implement IT to attack the problems of credibility. The strengthening of the credibility process relies on the use of a policy rule (Taylor type, for instance), which will become a reference for the behavior of the central bank and includes the rate of inflation, which will serve as the new nominal anchor.

To determine whether the Mexican central bank has intervened in the foreign exchange market, it is necessary to observe the behavior of international reserves and the performance of the exchange rate. The above will be made by calculating two indicators of volatility: the variance (σ^2) and the standard deviation (σ) of the exchange rate. This analysis is based on that performed by Zarate (2010) covering the period 1996:01–2009:08; the period was subdivided into three parts, and the results were as follows.

TABLE 4.2   Exchange Rate Volatility, 1996–2009

Indicator/Period	1996:01–2000:12	2001:01–2005:12	2006:01–2009:08
σ^2	0.8	0.7	1.6
σ	0.9	0.8	1.3

Source: Zárate, D., El trípode de Taylor. La teoría y una aplicación al caso mexicano, 2001–2009. Tesis de maestría. Facultad de Economía, Universidad Nacional Autónoma de México, 2010. With permission

It can be noted that in the first subperiod and the second, there were no significant changes in both indicators. However, in the third period of time, there is significant change with respect to the first and second periods, growth "which in large part is explained by the depreciation that occurred due to the global crisis that developed in the U.S. mortgage sector" (Zarate, 2010).

The initial observations of Calvo (1997) compared to the first period are as follows: *i*) the fiscal and monetary authorities assumed a posture essentially of financial crisis prevention; *ii*) defended the stability of exchange with high interest rates; *iii*) there were large differences between the rate of reference of Mexico (Certificados de la Tesoreria de la Federación [CETES] 91) and US Treasury bonds, which predicted a process of large devaluations; and *iv*) the expectations of devaluation were unstable. Concisely, the behavior of BANXICO was very adaptive through a market opened with the so-called "short" operations. Immediately, Table 4.3 is presented to evaluate the Calvo–Reinhart hypothesis for the period 2000–2011, which also suggests a subsection for better understanding.

TABLE 4.3   Exchange Rate Volatility, 2000–2011

Indicator/ Period	2000:01–2003:12	2004:01–2007:12	2008:01–2011:12
σ^2	0.43	0.06	1.29
σ	0.65	0.25	1.14

Source: Own elaboration base on Zárate, D. El trípode de Taylor. La teoría y una aplicación al caso mexicano, 2001-2009. Tesis de maestría. Facultad de Economía, Universidad Nacional Autónoma de México, 2010. With permission

This subdivision is raised this way because for the first period, it is known that since 2000, the Mexican issuing institution began publishing quarterly inflation reports and added the concept of core inflation as a determinant for the analysis of inflation. Subsequently, the process to improve transparency was reinforced in 2001, since it was in this year that the IT was officially adopted.

The second period was thus selected since 2003 defined a target for long-term inflation of 3%, with a range of variability, and the mechanism of the short was used during this period of time until the end of 2007. Finally, the third period was defined as well since in 2008, the Mexican Central Bank ceased to use the mechanism of the "short" and monetary policy went on to be orchestrated through an operational target defined by the interbank interest rate overnight. Also, during this period, the implications of the financial crisis that emerged in the US were included.

The results obtained show that the period that was analyzed as the Mexican economy's "fear to float" regime by Calvo, Reinhart, and Zarate in Mexico, people were under a dirty or managed floating exchange rate regime, since there is descending and indirect manipulation through constant interventions by the authorities. The authorities do not make explicit their desire for a specific value of the currency but they intervene to affect their behavior (tendency). The same is true of international reserves.

With regard to Boxes 4.1 and 4.2, I conclude that there is a difference in the calculation of the volatilities (variance and standard deviations), although different periods have been used for each analysis. However, in the last period of Table 4.2 (2008–2011), there is evidence that the volatility of the exchange rate during this period of time increased considerably due to the *subprime* crisis and its effects. These effects, in the case of Mexico, resulted in interventions in the foreign exchange market to maintain stable weight and parity against the dollar.

4.3   EVALUATION

For the evaluation of the IT, this section will be based on a test proposed by Svensson. In this way, there is a brief summary in Table 4.4 that shows that the Mexican Central Bank considers that potential inflationary pressures come as both demand shocks and supply shocks, and it suggests certain actions to be followed to counter such shocks.

Svensson[28] proposes a very simplified test to assess the credibility of the inflation targeting. A *test* of credibility is built through the subtraction of a maximum and a minimum of the rate of inflation that is consistent with the targets of inflation on the maturation of the nominal bond yields. The result of the above "is a consistent range of real nominal bonds against performance of target" (Svensson, 1993). The form of assessment, according to Svensson, is as follows: If the expected real yield or interest rate of the real bonds (if available) falls below the consistent range of target's performance, credibility is rejected.

---

[28]His academic career began at the University of Stockholm, Sweden, shortly after he obtained his Ph.D. in Economics in 1996. Years later, he was Professor at Princeton University, USA, until 2007, the year in which he was called to be a substitute Governor of the Sveriges Riskbank or the Central Bank of Sweden, which he had been managing since 1990.

TABLE 4.4   References to the Operation of Central Banks Under the Regime of Inflation Targeting

Source of Inflationary Pressures	Recommendation	Consequence
Demand	No accommodation of the shock effect	
Supply	Accommodate the shock so that the effect falls on the price level	First-round effects are recorded. However, if the effect contaminated inflation expectations, second-round price effects will emerge

Source: Ramos-Francia, M., and Torres, A. Reducing inflation through inflation targeting: the Mexican experience, Banco de México, Documentos de investigación núm. 2005-01, julio, 2005. With permission

When a central bank announces inflation targeting in the form of range, it makes it between a maximum and a minimum (constant or variant in time) linked with the future inflation rate. It is advisable to insist that if a target for inflation is credible, it means that the market players believe that future inflation will be located within the range of the target. Svensson (1993) distinguished two concepts about the credibility of the inflation targeting. A strong credibility, as an "absolute" concept, is when private agents are 100% sure that future inflation will be within the range of the target. This means that these agents are convinced that the probability of error of the target range is zero.

The second concept is the weak credibility and is referred to as "credibility in expectations" and refers to the situation in which the market players expect that the future value of the rate of inflation is located within the range of the target. In this case, the agents will know that there is some probability that the target fails. However, to test the credibility of a target for inflation, it is necessary to compute, for a given time horizon, future inflation rates' maximum and minimum, which are consistent with inflation targeting.[29]

In the *test* of 1993, Svensson establishes three versions that will be reviewed below. The first version has a market for real bonds. Here, a market

---

[29]As mentioned above, these maximum and minimum future inflation rates are subtracted from the nominal interest rate of government bonds in the corresponding term. The result is a consistent target with the actual maximum and minimum (about nominal bonds).

for the actual bonds is considered to be functioning, which has reliable figures on market for real interest rates. The *test* is to examine if the market of real interest rates, given a certain maturity, is between the minimum and the maximum of the actual performance of the consistent target. If the real market interest rate falls outside the range, then the "absolute credibility" is rejected. This is so because if there were absolute credibility, market players should believe that yields on the term associated on a nominal bond should have 100% probability of falling into the actual performance of the consistent target.[30]

However, if the actual market interest rate falls outside the range between the minimum and the maximum of the actual performance consistent target, coupled with a low inflation risk premium, it also rejects "credibility in expectations."[31] That is why an inflation risk premium means that yields expected on a nominal bond are approximately equal to the actual market interest rate. Now, given that the expected real returns associated with the maturity on a nominal bond are equal to the difference between the nominal yield and expected inflation (in the same term), it would be in the particular case where the expected inflation rate falls outside the range of target inflation.

Finally, the inflation risk premium is smaller under the "credibility of expectations." The inflation risk premium is determined by the conditional variance of the rate of inflation and the conditional variance between the inflation rate and other risks. Therefore, "it is likely that credibility in expectations is a small associated conditional variance and, consequently, to a small conditional variance of the rate of inflation. All of the above involves a small inflation risk premium" (Svensson, 1993). What Svensson wants to convey is that when real bonds' market interest rate expectations are located outside the range between minimum and maximum actual throughput of the consistent target of nominal bonds, not just the "absolute credibility" but also the credibility they enjoy should be rejected.[32]

---

[30]In this way, there might be a positive minimum safe gain. In this context, two situations can occur: *i*) the real bonds' market interest rate falls below the minimum actual performance of the consistent target of nominal bonds and *ii*) the real interest rate is located above the real maximum of the consistent target of nominal bonds.

[31]The inflation risk premium is the difference between expected real maturity associated with the nominal bond yield and the real rate of interest of market on a real bonus.

[32]Then, if the real interest rate falls between the minimum and maximum actual performance of the associated maturity, it does not mean that absolute credibility should be accepted, since it is not expected by market players that even some positive probability that the future inflation rate falls off the assigned target range may hold. "Credibility in expectations" should be accepted by the same argument but with reference to the inflation risk premium.

Svensson raises, in addition, a situation in which there is no market for the actual bonds. If there is a market with good performance for real bonds, there can be no security and certainty for real interest rates, and the test of credibility is not so simple. Then, it is useful to judge whether or not it is likely that private agents expect that the expected real returns are placed between the minimum and maximum actual performance of consistent target. Under this judgment, it is necessary to consider other types of information available (last real yields *ex post*). If it is very probable that the expected future performance falls outside the target range, then the "absolute credibility" and "credibility in expectations" must be rejected. The opposite happens if the expected future performance is located within the target with the caveat that you must not necessarily accept "absolute credibility."

Thus, the fundamental of this test is what Svensson called "real rate consistent with the target," which is defined as the difference between the nominal interest rate and the target for the inflation rate. For example, if the target of the rate of inflation for the next 3 years is 3% and the rate of interest for a period of 3 years is 6%, the real rate consistent with the target is 3%. If a rate is consistent with the target, it is also significantly higher than the expected real rate and suggests that the public is waiting for an inflation rate above the target range of the central bank, i.e., that the target of inflation is not credible. On the contrary, if the rate is consistent with the target, it is similar to the expected real rate and the target of inflation is said to be credible.

It should be noted that an unusually high rate of consistent target implies, if same, that the target of inflation is not credible even when the expected real rate is very similar. The presence of uncertainty causes lenders to demand a risk premium to cover the risks associated with inflation. Therefore, a considerable degree of uncertainty can lead to a very high inflation risk premium, which in turn, causes the rate of consistent target to become high even when the public is convinced that inflation will not exceed the target of the central bank. Below is a table that summarizes the above argument.

TABLE 4.5   Credibility of Inflation Targeting

Test	Case 1	Case 2	Case 3	With Uncertainty
Rate consistent with target[a]	High	Similar[b]	High	High[c]
Expected real rate	Slow	Similar[b]	High	High
Evaluation	Not credible	Credible	Not credible	Not credible

[a]Is the difference between the nominal interest rate and the target inflation rate.
[b]Similar but moderate.
[c]If the rate consistent with the target is high, then there refuses to be target credibility even when both rates are equal.

Source: Compilation based on Trehan, B. The credibility of inflation targeting, Federal Reserve Bank of San Francisco, Weekly Letter, N° 95-01, enero, 1995. With permission

As shown in Table 4.5, "a consistent target that is unusually high rate suggests that we should reject the credibility, even if this rate is the same as the expected real rate" (Trehan, 1995). To take this decision, it is essential to perform a trial, since the expected real rate is not observable; therefore, it is necessary to use a variable *proxy*. This variable is the real rate, which is built by subtraction of the current inflation (for the period) of the nominal interest rate that prevailed at the beginning of the period.

What is known regarding the credibility of the targets of inflation under the conditions of the test proposed by Svensson is that, based on the experiences of many countries with explicit targets, "for a target to become credible some time is necessary" (Trehan, 1995). Some economists argue that having targets and more explicit targets for inflation improves credibility. However, "others say that credibility is gained by showing that the central bank is willing to take the steps necessary to first achieve and then maintain low inflation" (Judd, 1995).

In the next chapter, four scenarios describe the credibility of the target of inflation in Mexico. The choice of the periods of analysis is explained in subsection C of Chapter 5. Then, the target of inflation in Mexico that will be evaluated is defined by a permanent target of 3%, which can vary by ±1%, whose assessment will apply to target spot. For the application of the *test* proposed by Svensson, following series of monthly data were necessary: annualized inflation was necessary for inflation consistent with the target and series of CETES 28 days was used for nominal bonds.

The evaluation is applied on the basis of the existence of a market of real bonds in functioning, which has reliable figures on the market for real interest rates. Thus, to obtain the range or ranges, it was necessary to detect the maximum and the minimum inflation rates of each. Once we had an interval, we calculated the rate of real return. This rate is the result of the subtraction between the average performances of the rate for CETES 28 days less the average rate of inflation for each period. Thus, we present the results obtained in Table 4.6, in which are recorded the intervals corresponding to the four mentioned study periods called *subsamples*, the actual performance of the nominal variable used, and finally, the opinion of the evaluation.

TABLE 4.6 Evaluation of the Credibility of the Inflation Targeting for Mexico, 2001–2012

Subsamples	Interval	Real Yield CETES 28 days)	Evaluation
2001:01–2003:03	(1.89–9.78)	3.48	Accepted the credibility
2003:04–2005:03	(1.15–2.43)	2.59	Not accepted the credibility[a]
2005:04–2007:12	(4.97–5.15)	3.94	Not accepted the credibility
2008:01–2012:07	(1.23–3.72)	0.86	Not accepted the credibility

[a]The result indicates that the actual performance is located above the range. It is above the range minimally, which is evidence that it rejects both credibility as well as the expectations credibility.

Source: Homemade

As you can see, the first period assessment is positive, since the credibility of the IT is accepted. In this case are accepted both types of credibility, the absolute as well as the credibility of expectations since the performance of the real nominal variable fell within the range. However, in the following subsamples, nominal variable performance did not fall within the respective ranges, as definitely as said by Svensson, rejecting the two types of credibility, both the strong and the weak.

The test proposed by Svensson says that it is likely that for countries with explicit targets, time may be needed before any monetary policy proposals can be made credible. However, the results for the previous year establish an opposite pattern. I mean that in the first period, the inflation targeting was credible, and in my opinion, it could be due to the need of the issuing institution to generate certainty at the start of the formal adoption of the IT. Therefore, variables such as inflation and rate for CETES 28 days were controlled and focused, respectively.

Little credibility observed from the second period is also evidence of a process deviation of the rate of interest from that of the USA, which is clearly a reference to countries like Mexico and, in general, the central banks of the world. They note that in the second period, extending to 2005, begins the trend that caused the result that very little credibility according to this test is accepted. Then, in the third and fourth subperiods, it can be seen that the actual performance with which we are working is, by far, the most raised range, which makes us think that, effectively, the diversion begins to become more severe and marked, which generated uncertainty in private agents in the USA first and, later, for those in Mexico.

So, it is concluded that uncertainty of compliance with the target of inflation rests on the reputation and credibility of the central bank. So, deviating from the raised issues is a very delicate issue since agents "are easily scared" and show that nervousness in the short and medium term results in loss of reputation and credibility. What should be done , in general terms, is to obtain the raised target and warn ahead of time a change or modification in the stance of monetary policy to avoid mismatches in expectations of private economic agents.

KEYWORDS

- BANXICO,
- International reserves,
- Transmission mechanism,
- Calvo–Reinhart hypothesis,
- Fear of floating,
- Credibility in expectations

CHAPTER 5

MEXICO: POLICY RULES, 2001–2012

CONTENTS

For those emerging market economies that do not choose a policy of "permanently" fixing the exchange rate – perhaps through a currency board of dollarization, the only sound monetary policy is one based on the trinity of a flexible exchange rate, an inflation targeting, and a monetary policy rule.

—John B. Taylor, 2000

Mexico is a country with a small and open economy. In this type of countries has been observed an evolution, in what refers to monetary policy, which can be described using the estimation of an augmented Taylor rule and, in specific, this is so in the case of Mexico. "The determinants of the real interest rate included in this analysis are deviating from expected inflation of the objective of the central bank, a measure of the output gap, using for its construction, industrial production, the rate of monetary of the run-up and the interest rate on public debt denominated in foreign currency" (Ortiz, 2000). As reviewed later, Svensson (1998) has developed a model with rational expectations and that included a function of reaction, which responds to variables such as the rate of inflation, the output gap, the interest rate, and the real and external exchange rates. The results obtained by Ortiz (2000) for the period from May 1997 to May 2000 show that the real ex-ante rate of interest responded strongly and significantly to changes in the external interest rate and the depreciation of exchange in the previous month.

During this period, Ortiz said that the rate of interest considerably responded to external events, limiting the pressures arising from changes in the exchange rate. It is important to establish that from May 1997 to November 1998, a considerable disorder in the international financial markets was raised because of the Asian and Russian crises. These events were the main sources of volatility on interest rates denominated in foreign currency and the exchange rate of emerging countries.

On the contrary, the period from December 1998 to May 2000 was characterized by a greater stability in the international financial markets. Then, without major external shocks, once the transition to the targets of inflation (officially the Banco de México [BANXICO] adopted inflation targeting in 2001) was completed, the relative importance of the factors that determine the real interest rate was reversed. This means, deviating from its inflation target took greater importance as a determinant of the real interest rate, while the external interest rate and the rate of depreciation lost importance in the same category.[1]

In the case of Mexico, the effect of the interest rate on aggregate demand would be taking greater relevance. In this way, it would be possible to take the interest rate as the main instrument of monetary policy, provided the aforementioned structural changes have been carried out and thus reduce the importance of the transmission of the exchange rate channel to monetary policy.

5.1   THE APPROACH OF THE BANXICO

The process of determination of the interest rates in Mexico is relevant for our purposes. It is useful to formally test whether under a flexible exchange rate regime, monetary policy instrument has served as a nominal anchor for the economy. With a default exchange rate, monetary policy is restricted to exchange rate variations and only dedicates itself to support exchange-rate policy. Under these circumstances, monetary policy is only instrumental. Conversely, a scheme of free floating monetary policy is not limited by the exchange conditions of the country and, therefore, central banks are responsible for formulating monetary policy that ensures price stability.[2]

Garcia (2002) points out that an economy as small and open as the Mexican is exposed to the volatility of international financial markets; this variability affects the structure of interest rates in the world, but specifically in emerging markets. Added to that there were internal factors that made it difficult, in the implementation of monetary policy, and one element to be considered in the formation of inflation back expectations. Therefore, this way of forming expectations makes it difficult to reduce inflation to the central bank.[3]

Then again the rules *versus* discretion debate modified the tendency of how to make monetary policy, limiting the discretionary effort through

---

[1]Thus concludes Ortiz (2000) for the Mexican case, in the second period of limited volatility and transition to the IT, interest rates were responding more significantly to aggregate demand and inflationary pressures that had their origin in domestic market.

[2]Under these last conditions, monetary policy not only serves as an instrumental role, since it is responsible for choosing the operating mechanisms that lead it to serve as the nominal anchor of the economy.

[3]A factor to consider is the effect of the exchange rate depreciation on prices when these are considered permanent.

the use of flexible monetary policy rules. This gave antecedent to set inflation targeting. The inflation-targeting approach (IT) considers maintaining low and stable inflation as its main objective. Thus, under a framework of stability emerges the Taylor *tripod*, which is one of the most current and accepted of monetary policies by many countries, both developed and emerging.

In this context, Mexico began a series of transformations since the crisis of 1994, among which are the following: the independence of the central bank, the transition to flexible exchange rate regime, and the adoption of IT. The provision of autonomy of the issuing institution sought to provide full freedom for the implementation of monetary policy to achieve inflation targeting. Obviously, monetary policies can be discretionary; however, it is also possible to identify some regular or systematic behavior that can be modeled by rules. This type of monetary policy instruments allows assessing the preferences of the central bank in its decisions with respect to variables such as inflation or economic growth.[4]

The use of monetary rules represents a guide for decision making of the issuing institution for developed countries; however, for developing or emerging countries, it is difficult to define accurately the systematic component of monetary policy, that is, what is the form of nominal anchor of the economy. In the Mexican case, BANXICO's main objective is to maintain low and stable inflation rates. This is a fundamental thesis that this work intends to verify.

The rules of monetary policy also can be understood as functions of reaction; therefore, it is possible to check the interaction between monetary policy and other variables that influence the actions of central banks, and this means a country's macroeconomic performance is closely linked to monetary policy decisions.

In addition, the analysis of monetary policy rules is essential in those countries whose system is based on the IT. Thus, there is a partial consensus on the debate between rules and discretion, in which rules emerge as a mechanism that narrows the discretion of authorities, and so are preferred with regard to those policies that deviate. This is because, usually, the latter are inconsistent over time since they generate a problem of "inflationary bias."

---

[4]A central bank does not necessarily define how explicit a rule is to the period of management. The rules, in addition to simulating the behavior of historical actions of central banks, also allow approximating the path of so-called optimal monetary policy.

The Taylor (1993) document is relevant since it pioneered the exemplification of the methodology of policy rules. According to Taylor (1993, 1999) a monetary policy rule is a "contingency plan that specifies as clearly as possible the circumstances under which a central bank should change the instruments of monetary policy." In this way, "The Taylor rule aims to describe the function of reaction from the central bank to the (differential) evolution of inflation and the product" (Galindo and Guerrero, 2003).

Thus, "the first step to design a monetary policy rule is to choose the instrument," i.e., the variable that will be used as an instrument to achieve the objective of the central bank. Subsequently, the issuing institution selects the variables that would react, or those that could modify its stance of monetary policy, beforehand. The Taylor rule reacts to variations in inflation as the product; thus, "variations in the rate of interest not only represent the actions of the central bank but via their effect on expected aggregate demand, although showing lag, influence the behavior of inflation and of the product" (Torres, 2002).

An important aspect with respect to the monetary rule of Taylor is that it includes the output gap. Thus, if the basic objective of the issuing institution is the stability of prices, it will react only to variabilities of the inflation gap: "this situation has been called inflation targeting in the extreme (*extreme inflation targeting*)" (Torres, 2002). The damage caused by this approach so far is that the real sector of the economy is more vulnerable to temporary supply disruptions.[5] On the other hand, when the output gap is included in the rule of monetary policy reaction function, the effect of a temporary shock on real activity in the economy is less.[6]

One clear advantage that Torres (2002) traced with respect to the use of rules that react to both gaps is that this ensures that only temporary shocks have first-order effects on prices, and constant or recurring inflationary pressures can be eliminated by increasing the interest rate. In his 2002 paper, Torres indicates that authors like Svensson (1996) and Clarida, Galí, and Gertler (1999) formalized the theoretical foundations of the Taylor rule. However, these authors did not formalize the issues raised by Taylor; what they did was to formalize the modifications that were brought about to the original rule of 1993.

---

[5] When inflationary pressures arise from the demand side, derived from excess spending, monetary policy reacts by increasing the rate of interest in the effect of both gaps.
[6] When increases in temporary prices of inputs are unavailable, the increase in the rate of interest suggested by the inflation gap is offset by the reduction in interest rates suggested by the decrease of the output gap.

Thus, the models of the authors mentioned in the previous paragraph are approximations to the Taylor rule through a process of optimization, in which the issuing institution minimizes a loss function that is quadratic in the inflation gap and can be the output gap and that the result is a version of the forward-looking monetary rule (*forward looking*). Torres (2002) presents the following:

$$i_t = \alpha + \beta\left(E_t\left[\pi_{t+n} - \pi^*\right]\right) + \gamma\left(E_t\left[y_{t+k} - y_{t+k}^*\right]\right), \qquad (5.1)$$

where

π_{t+n} : is the inflation between period t and the period $t + n$,

y_{t+k} : is the product of the products t and $t + k$, and
E_t: is the operator's expectations that form with the information available in the period t.

Then, the performance of monetary policy (Mexican) is based on the *expected behavior* of inflation and product gaps. The above is a clear rule raised by Torres and responds to the expected performance of the gaps, and not the observed (past and present) ones, as proposed by the Taylor (1993) rule. For this, it is necessary to review the issues raised in the first two paragraphs of Chapter 3 of this research. The relevance and, therefore, the utility – that is, the interpretation of the rules to understand monetary policy – lies in the analysis of the coefficients β and γ.

The first one (β) shows the aggressiveness of the response from the central bank to deviations of inflation with respect to its objective. Considering that α represents the equilibrium real interest rate in the long run, monetary policy rule can be expressed in the following way:

$$r_t = \bar{r} + (\beta-1)\times\left(E_t\left[\pi_{t+n}\right] - \pi^*\right) + \gamma\left(E_t\left[y_{t+k} - y_{t+k}^*\right]\right), \quad (5.2)$$

where r_t is the short-term real interest rate and $\bar{r}$ is the level of long-term real interest rate.

Equation (5.2) shows that the critical value for the parameter β is one, since in the event that inflation expectations will rise above its target, i.e., the parameter $\beta > 1$, the monetary policy rule implies that the central bank increase the rate of nominal interest (i_t) enough to raise the real rate of interest (r_t). This would lead to a contraction in aggregate demand and would push inflation expectations to converge to its objective. On the other hand, when $\beta < 1$, the increase in the nominal interest rate will not be enough to induce an increase of the real interest rate. In fact, in this case, the real interest rate decreases, since the increase in the nominal interest rate is lower than the increase observed in the expectation of inflation ($E_t[\pi_{t+n}]$). In this way, aggregate demand is encouraged, negative to the stance of monetary policy, affecting inflation expectations.

Now, a monetary policy rule as in equation (5.1), with $\beta > 1$, as proposed by Torres (2002), works automatically to stabilize inflation around its target. When this happens, it is said that monetary policy is consistent with the IT. This happens in the following way: when inflation expectations are diverted from their objective, the central bank acts to induce the convergence of expected inflation in order, which means that monetary policy effectively constitutes the nominal anchor of the economy.

With respect to the parameter γ, equations (5.1) and (5.2) show that its threshold is zero. To illustrate how, this product level is assumed to be located above its potential level ($E_t[y_{t+k} - y_{t+k}^*] > 0$). Then, if $\gamma > 0$, the response of the central banker "is nominal and real interest rate increases to prevent the diversion of the products with respect to its potential level to generate future pressures on inflation" (Torres, 2002). Then, to the contrary, when $\gamma < 0$, rule-oriented monetary policy reductions in nominal and real interest rates lead to increase of aggregate demand, which in turn increases the product, eventually resulting in greater lowering of inflation rates.

For Torres (2002), if this rule of monetary policy is governed by and meets two fundamental guidelines, $\beta > 1$ and $\gamma \geq 0$, then the monetary rule is effectively the nominal anchor of the economy. Now, since this analysis is based on small and open economies such as that of Mexico, the work of Ball (1999) and Svensson (2000) suggests that for this type of market, rules of monetary policy – as well as inflation and product gaps – should be their other variables.[7] One of the variables that these last two authors propose to be included in the monetary policy rule is the "external

---

[7] These variables are most useful in that they capture the pressures of future inflation faster than inflation and product gaps making it on their own.

interest rate."[8] Other variables can be included to have as the basic objective shaping of monetary conditions with several policy instruments.

This then is the example of monetary rule that includes the exchange rate; thus "monetary conditions are modeled as a combination between the levels of the interest rate and the exchange rate" (Torres, 2002)

$$i_t = \alpha + \beta(E_t[\pi_{t+n} - \pi^*]) + \gamma(E_t[y_{t+k} - y^*_{t+k}]) + \varphi(E_t[z_{t+m}]), \quad (5.3)$$

where z_{t+m} represents the set of variables that could possibly influence the stance of monetary policy, such as the type of change, external interest rates, sovereign risk, etc.

There are other authors who have reviewed the situation of small and open economies, such as Clarida et al. (2001), and they arrive at conclusions such as that the optimal monetary policy rule is equal to that specified for the case of a closed economy (see equation 5.1) at the same time. According to these authors, the only feature that differs is that "the effect of the relevant variables in an open economy... on inflation is captured by the parameters of the rule" (Torres, 2002). This means that the difference in involvement level is quantitative, i.e., the magnitude of the parameters β and γ, the interest rate, as well as the inflation and product gap. This means that the opening up of the economy affects the parameters of the model but not the general form of the optimal monetary policy rule.

Then, according to Torres (2002), if variations in the type of change or external interest rates affect expected inflation and the expected product, the central bank will react to the exchange rate volatilities and external interest rates.[9] Conversely, one should not modify monetary policy if it is considered that the fluctuations of variables, such as the exchange rate and external interest rates, do not affect inflation.

Referring to the Mexican case, since the adoption of the flexible exchange in 1994, the BANXICO has designated the nominal interest rate as the nominal anchor of the economy. To test this, members of the Mexican central bank engaged in research have proposed evaluation of the parameter β, and if this is greater that one, it then formally proves that the instrument of monetary policy has been established as the anchor and not as that

---

[8]The concept of external interest rate is introduced since variations of this on inflation are not always immediately observable in the gaps of inflation and product.

[9]To assess the effect of variables other than inflation and the product on the implementation of monetary policy in Mexico. In the case of an economy that is small and open as the Mexican, it is suitable to formally test the role of variables as the amount of money, the exchange rate, sovereign risk, and the differential of domestic interest rates in the short and long terms.

proposed by Torres (2002). He says that if this parameter is greater that unity, the BANXICO is the nominal anchor, and this is a wrong statement.

On the other hand, Torres (2002) argues that monetary policy in Mexico is facing a front that is *forward looking* in nature, as known in the literature of monetary policies. It argues that this is a key element of the IT, formally adopted by the Mexican central institution in 2001. Consistency of monetary policy that looks forward with inflation targeting is determined simply by comparing with one that looks back (*looking backward*). We are convinced that the above assertion is incorrect, or at least incomplete, since we believe that it is not as simple as Torres puts it in his 2002 paper.[10]

For the specification of the basic monetary rule, Torres (2002) carried out an identification of factors that meet the needs of liquidity from the money market. In the case of Mexico, this identification is not simple, since the BANXICO did not conduct beforehand a survey to determine the level of the reference interest rates. Then, when the central institution wanted to change the stance of monetary policy, it did affect market conditions, through the modification of the current account of commercial banks with the central bank (remuneration of deposits and overdraft facilities), allowing the precise level of the interest rate to be determined by the market.

When the above is not enough and the rate of interest determined by the market is not consistent with the approach of BANXICO inflation targeting, then this changed market conditions again to "convenience" until the rate set by the supply and demand is consistent with the intentions of the central bank. Therefore, even though the Mexican central bank does not directly set the interest rate, its level is compatible with the stance of monetary policy and therefore says Alberto Torres, the interest rate is also an instrument of monetary policy.

Thus, Torres (2002) established that an optimal monetary policy rule can be defined as follows:

$$i_t^* = \left(K + \alpha\pi_{t+n}^*\right) + \beta\left(E_t\left[\pi_{t+n} - \pi_{t+n}^*\right]\right) + \gamma\left(E_t\left[y_{t+k} - y_{t+k}^*\right]\right), \quad (5.4)$$

where

i_t^* : is the goal of the optimum nominal interest rate (optimal monetary instrument level) and

---

[10]Not enough comparisons between the components looking back and looking forward are available to determine whether monetary policy is consistent with the IT.

$K + \alpha \pi^*_{t+n}$: is the long-term nominal interest rate.

It is important to note that the long-term nominal interest rate $(K + \alpha \pi^*_{t+n})$ and the inflation target (π^*_{t+n}) are not constant over time. According to Torres (2002), this is due to the fact that the Mexican economy has undergone a process of disinflation, in which inflation targeting set by the BANXICO has continued a downward slide. In the practical field, Clarida et al. (1998, 2000) argue that the behavior of central banks is to adjust interest rates gradually. In this way, the monetary authority determines the rate of interest (i_t) as a weighted average of the optimal interest rate (i^*_t) and the interest rate observed in the previous period (i_{t-1}), more an exogenous term of disturbances at the rate of interest with zero mean[11]

$$ i_t = \left(1 - \rho\right) i^*_t + \rho i_{t-1} + v_t. \tag{5.5} $$

Here the parameter ρ ranges between zero and one and measures the gradualism that interest rates are adjusted. Finally, the combination of the last two equations yields the basic specification of the monetary rule used to estimate the Mexican economy, according to Torres (2002), and is described below:

$$ i_t = (1-\rho)\left(K + \alpha\pi^*_{t+n}\right) + (1-\rho)\beta\left(E_t\left[\pi_{t+n} - \pi^*_{t+n}\right]\right) + (1-\rho)\gamma\left(E_t\left[y_{t+k} - y^*_{t+k}\right]\right) + \rho i_{t-1} + v_t. \tag{5.6} $$

In the case of Mexican economy, expectations of inflation, in 2002, relied exclusively on the market, so it was normal to get incorrect results. Therefore, if the market's inflation expectations rise proportionately less than the increase by the issuing institution, the parameter β estimating inflation forecasts would be lower than that calculated using estimates of the central bank. This would lead to the situation that the monetary authority would carry out an increase less than the interest rate to fight inflation.

An additional aspect that hinders the estimation of equation (5.6) is that the information about the output gap is not accurate, and its calculation was the subject of many controversies. For this reason, BANXICO is based on the documents for 1998, 1999, and 2000 of Clarida et al., where the generalized method of moments is suggested as a methodology for the

---

[11]These disturbances measure the effect of unexpected changes to adjustments in interest rates that are not based on the fundamentals of the economy or monetary policy.

estimation of equation (5.6). To explain this method, equation (5.6) is expressed in the following way, where the output gap is replaced by (x_{t+k}):

$$i_t = (1-\rho)(K + \alpha\pi_{t+n}^*) + (1-\rho)\beta(E_t[\pi_{t+n} - \pi_{t+n}^*]) + (1-\rho)\gamma(x_{t+k}) + \rho i_{t-1} + \varepsilon_t. \quad (5.7)$$

The error term is defined here as follows:

$$\varepsilon_t = v_t - (1-\rho)\beta\{(\pi_{t+n} - \pi_{t+n}^*) - E_t[\pi_{t+n} - \pi_{t+n}^*]\} - (1-\rho)\gamma(x_{t+k} - E_t[x_{t+k}]). \quad (5.8)$$

And it is a linear combination of the exogenous disturbance (v_t), monetary policy, and forecasting errors. Equation (5.7) uses values observed *ex post* of the gap of inflation and the product. Therefore, the obtained estimators are unbiased estimators for parameters α, β, γ, and ρ, provided the forecast errors are zero. The generalized method of moments ensures that forecast errors are zero by information contained in a set of variables (U_t) known from the period t when determining the interest rate i_t.[12]

However, this strategy places orthogonal restrictions that are used by the generalized method of moments to estimate the parameters α, β, γ, and ρ given by $E[\varepsilon_t | U_t] = 0$. It is important to note that when the number of variables included in U_t (instruments) is greater than the number of variables to estimate, the model is said to be unidentified. Once revised, the specification and the methodology for estimating raised some issues, which, for this research, are devoid of foundations, are erroneous, or are presented so that they are suitable for the author to read according to the interests of the same.

The first one refers to the fact that Torres (2002) states that the BANXI-CO played the role of nominal anchor of the economy in 1994. This turns out to be inaccurate, since the role of anchor must comply with precisely being a nominal variable and not an institution or a policy of any institution. In this case, you must specify a policy that includes in its structure a certain nominal variable that serves as an instrument to carry out its role.

The following graphs (Figure 5.1) were used to test the hypothesis of whether monetary policy has played the role of nominal anchor of the Mexican economy. Once more, the above statement is inaccurate by what was said in the previous paragraph.

---

[12]The instrumental variable (U_t) includes lags in all those variables that are useful for forecasting inflation and product gaps.

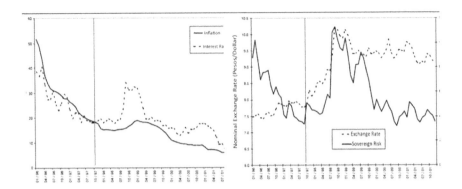

FIGURE 5.1   Inflation, Interest Rate, Sovereign Risk, and Exchange Rate.
Source: (Own; From Torres, A. Un análisis de las tasas de interés en México a través de
la metodología de reglas monetarias, Documento de investigación núm. 2002-11, Banco de
México, diciembre, 2002. With permission.)

Cutting is noticeable in both panels in October 1997. The objection
that this document takes place at the above period refers to the first panel,
which shows the inflation and interest rate and note that from the chart, the
relationship between them is negative; this means that when the interest
rate increases, inflation is reduced. This suggests that the nominal variable
(interest rate) has successfully served the role of nominal anchor of the
Mexican economy. Or that when BANXICO raised interest rates, it took
inflation to low levels. The BANXICO tested this hypothesis, since it considers the rule of basic monetary policy described by equation (5.6), to see
whether the parameter β is statistically greater than one.

Without a doubt, the right panel associated sovereign risk with the exchange rate. In this combination of variables and, according to the graph,
it appears that when the exchange rate increases (it depreciates or devalues
the domestic currency), country risk increases. Also, in the more recent
periods, it can be observed that when the exchange rate is stable, sovereign
risk is considerably reduced. The objective of both panels is met perfectly
(according to the objectives of the author); however, there is an additional
relationship that can be deduced from the previous chart so, a much more
thorough analysis of the previous associations should be carried out.

The relationship that is intended to be demonstrated is that which involves the sovereign risk and the interest rate. What we want to show here
is that the interest rate, used by the Mexican central bank as a monetary

policy instrument, is not only more correlated with inflation, but that the association is positive in nature. For this reason, a brief discussion of the implications of the relationship hidden from both halves of the previous chart follows. The main implication emanating from the previous assertion is that the nominal anchor of the economy is not exactly the nominal instrument of the central bank, much less the monetary policy of the same. What can be deduced from the variable interest rate and country risk is that when the interest rate of the Mexican economy increases, the risk of investing in Mexico rises, or at least that is the perception of the countries abroad. Therefore, the possibility to include additional variables in the monetary policy rule is validated with certain coherence. Otherwise, it would suffice to simply have a rule of monetary policy such as the one posed by Taylor in 1993, which includes only inflation and product gaps.

An additional element that is a cause of disputes is the period analyzed. I again argue that this frequency was chosen for the specific purposes that the author sought. However, as asserted by Torres (2002), the view that the increase in the rate of interest is what kept inflation at low levels is inaccurate because if you take it as a sign prior to cutting (October 1997), it could have behaved differently to the raised interest rate. What could be concluded would be that while the interest rate is reduced, then the inflation also makes it. This is completely opposite to the fact that the nominal variable (interest rate) monetary policy meets the role of nominal anchor of the Mexican economy.

As reviewed earlier and knowing the above, the part that follows is to establish the variables that were used by the staff of the BANXICO for the estimation of monetary policy specified by equation (5.6) rule, which were as follows:

i_t : Government funding, defined as the monthly average rate till date on the money market.

Inflation is defined as the percentage change from the National Index of Consumer Prices (Indice Nacional de Precios al Consumidor; INPC) during the previous 12 months. For its part, "it is monthly inflation targeting constructed using the annual goal announced by the Banco de México" (Torres, 2002). Now to the expectation of the output gap $(E_t[y_t - y_t^*])$, which is obtained by the output gap observed *ex post* $(y_t - y_t^*)$. Finally, the variable used for the monthly product is the overall global index of economic activity (Index of Global Economic Activity [Indicador Global de la Actividad Económica] or IGAE) and the potential product is obtained through a quadratic trend (this also was estimated using the Hodrick–Prescott filter).

The estimation of equation (5.7), which is the basic specification of the monetary policy rule, was performed by Torres (2002) using the generalized method of moments for three sets of instruments U_t. The first set includes remnants of the inflation gap $(\pi_{t-j} - \pi^*_{t-j})$, the product (x_{t-j}), and the interest rate gap (i_{t-j}). It is important to note that this first group of instruments only includes those variables that make up the essential structure of the rule of monetary policy raised by John Taylor in his paper of 1993. This is relevant because the two other groups suggested by Torres in 2002 added variables, which, according to the evidence presented, affect the determination of the interest rates in Mexico.

In this way, the remaining groups of instruments include in addition to the above variables an extra pair that affect inflation and which are useful for its forecast. Therefore, the second set includes the variable nominal wages lagging behind manufacturing industry (w_t), while the latter includes remnants of the nominal rate of Exchange (s_t). This suggests that three different estimates, which were described by the aforementioned instrument sets, were obtained. Therefore, the most relevant result is this: for sets two and three, it is concluded that instruments incorporated into the specification of the monetary rule are appropriate and that, therefore, wage and exchange rate serve to predict product and inflation expectations, so these latter variables in models incorporated in set two or three improve monetary rule setting, says Torres (2002).

Without a doubt, the result that Torres wanted to get is the determination of the nominal anchor of the economy, specifically whether "monetary policy" serves this role. To do this, it is necessary to review the magnitude of the parameter β since when this "is greater than one, monetary rule implies that when expected inflation is above the inflation targeting, the nominal interest rate increases enough to induce an increase in the real interest rate" (Torres, 2002). This is the way to determine if indeed the instrument of monetary policy (nominal interest rate) has been established as the nominal anchor of the economy.

An additional outcome that aims to validate the previous one is that when interest rates lead to the path of the product, it is placed around its potential level, preventing the emergence of permanent inflationary pressures. This reinforces the hypothesis that the actions of the BANXICO through its instrument of monetary policy have been established as the nominal anchor of the economy. This type of monetary policy rules describe that the interest rate is based on the behavior of the expectations of inflation and the product. However, "it is possible in a small and open economy like the Mexican to consider additional variables to obtain a specification that best describes the behavior of interest rates" (Torres, 2002).

To do this, the BANXICO, through its staff, presented "augmented" monetary policy rules that seek to establish what macroeconomic variables other than inflation and the product have influenced the formation of interest rates in Mexico. This type of rule is specified in the following manner:

$$i_t^* = \left(k + \alpha\pi_{t+n}^*\right) + \beta\left(E_t\left[\pi_{t+n} - \pi_{t+n}^*\right]\right) + \gamma\left(E_t\left[y_{t+k} - y_{t+k}^*\right]\right) + \varphi(E_t[z_{t+m}]). \tag{5.9}$$

The only thing that remains to be defined is z_{t+m}, which is the product, and any other variable, except inflation, considered to get the inflation targeting. Now if the equation is combined with equation (5.5), the estimated monetary policy rule is as follows:

$$i_t = (1-\rho)\left(K + \alpha\pi_{t+n}^*\right) + (1-\rho)\beta\left(E_t\left[\pi_{t+n} - \pi_{t+n}^*\right]\right) + (1-\rho)\gamma\left(E_t\left[y_{t+k} - y_{t+k}^*\right]\right) + (1-\rho)\varphi\left(E_t\left[z_{t+m}\right]\right) + \rho i_{t-1} + v_t. \tag{5.10}$$

Here, the variable z_{t+m} is defined in various ways. Monetary policy in Mexico since the adoption of inflation targeting is of a forward-looking character; this means that decisions are made based on the expected performance of the economy. Therefore, inflation expectations have greater relevance in determining interest rates and consequently inflation lagging increasingly is less relevant. In 2002, Torres's work tested if the interest rates are determined forward through the estimation of the rule of monetary policy increase described by equation (5.10), defining the variable z_{t+m} as the backlog of the inflation gap and knowing that the parameter m is equal to -1.

He concluded from the above that the process whereby the interest rates are determined in Mexico is built on the "forward looking" model, which was deduced since the parameter β is statistically greater than one and the parameter φ is not statistically different from zero. The implication of this result, according to Torres (2002), is that the increase in the nominal interest rate leads to an increase in the real interest in response to the expected inflation rate and not inflation.

As part of the increase in communication strategy, the BANXICO published a forecast of the monetary base since 1997. This release aims to help private economic actors to orient their expectations of inflation. It should be noted that this forecast is not a goal and, therefore, the actions of the central bank are not in order to achieve this objective. Equation (5.10) includes the variable monetary base used to meet the requirement to be able to term this equation increased monetary rule.

In this case, z_{t+m} represents the deviation of the monetary base with respect to its forecast in the previous period $(mb_{t-1} - mb_{t-1}^{f})$. The key result of this estimate is presented below: deviations from the monetary base with respect to its forecast do not influence the determination of the interest rates in Mexico. This led to Torres (2002) affirming that monetary policy has been conducted in the context of the IT and not with the objectives of monetary aggregates.

Theoretically, it is assumed that the nominal interest rate and the exchange rate are related. This partnership increases in small, open economies because of the connection between the money market and the exchange rate. Relevant search results show that variations in the exchange rate are positively related to the nominal interest rate (such deviations also are statistically significant). This suggests that part of the information contained in the nominal exchange rate is captured by inflation and product gaps. This causes (the inclusion of the nominal exchange rate) the parameter φ to downplay the parameters β and γ.[13]

The above analysis leads us to ask about the other part of the Taylor stand referring to the tip of the IT. Although we mentioned something about it, particularly the strategy of increasing communication between those responsible for monetary policy and private economic operators, it is

---

[13]However, a specification of the monetary rule, which in addition to including the inflation gap, includes the rate of exchange is not a proper representation of the process of formation of the interest rates in Mexico.

necessary to lead in all areas involving such an approach for the achievement of best in its management of monetary policy. For this reason, we will then review the Mexican experience of reducing inflation by inflation targeting.

Ramos and Torres (2005) say that in an economy that has managed to have a sustainable fiscal position, inflation targeting is an efficient mechanism to impose discipline on monetary policy and, therefore, reduce inflation in a systematic way. The trend toward flexible exchange rate accompanied by recommendations of IT (appropriate responses to inflationary shocks and transparency in their implementation) are decisive to run monetary policy as the nominal anchor of the economy. "Answers from the BANXICO to different inflation *shocks*, after the 1995 crisis,[14] were consistent with inflation-targeting approach principles." (Ramos-France and Torres, 2005)

From 1995, the BANXICO defined the rate of interest as the main instrument to effect a target for the current accounts of the cumulative balance of commercial banks with the central bank (short). Through the short interest rates, the criminalization of the overdraft of accounts of commercial banks can be affected. Subsequent to this was conducted the process characterized by the position of the BANXICO revised in part (rules of monetary policy and determination of interest rates in Mexico) before and, since both Ramos and Torres are officials, share fully the position assumed by the central institution.

This is the way in which the Mexican central bank operated through the instrument called "short." In 1995 and 1996, the instrument was amended many times within a very small range, some of them to make it more restrictive and others to ease monetary policy. These changes are to be seen, according to Torres and Ramos, as actions to influence interest rates for a very short time horizon and specifically to restore order in financial markets. In 1998, the possibility of fiscal dominance had disappeared and allowed the BANXICO to use a *forward-looking* monetary policy to combat inflation.

---

[14]The crisis was caused, according to Torres and Ramos-France, by the following: *i*) because the fixed exchange caused large speculative short-term capital inflows and a considerable distortion in prices, *ii*) weak monitoring and banking regulation that made management of flows of capital inefficient, *iii*) excessive spending and a huge current account deficit, and *iv*) as a result of the worsening macroeconomics, the Government was forced to restructure its debt in short-term securities denominated in dollars. All these circumstances interacted, causing an imbalance in the economy and, eventually, a run against the local currency.

Torres and Ramos emphasize three episodes in which "restricted" monetary policy goes hand in hand with the transition toward IT. Each of these situations presents something in common. To begin with, in every episode, the *short* was increased on many occasions, signaling a much more restrictive stance. Secondly, both the nominal and the real interest rate recorded upward trend in the three events, and the third feature that the above situations share is that the three announcements of monetary policy determined changes in the instrument, but specifically describe the shocks that the Mexico Bank was attending to in the process of disinflation.

In the first episode (1998:01–1999:03), increased inflationary pressures originated from an increase in the perception of sovereign risk and the depreciation of the peso caused by the financial crises in other emerging markets (Asia in 1997, Russia in 1998, and Brazil in early 1999). The second episode covers the period 2000:01–2001:01. During this period of time, inflationary pressures grew mainly by the rapid expansion of aggregate demand coming from the demand of the US and Mexican exports. Finally, the third period covers the period 2002:09–2003:03, which was characterized by a sharp increase in public as well as residential electricity prices.

During the incidence of these episodes of restrictive monetary policy, it was detected that the first and third events were characterized by a tendency toward a gap between expectations of rising inflation and a trend of the output gap. This suggests that the pressures on inflation came essentially from costs, i.e., from the supply side. However, in the second episode, both the output gap as well as a rising trend of the inflation was recorded, which allows one to think that the pressures arose from the demand side. Ramos and Torres (2005) conclude that the restrictive monetary policy during the three episodes revised was consistent with the IT.[15]

Now, the literature of inflation targeting allows establishing two key references for central banks: *i*) when inflationary pressures come from demand shocks, the recommendation is to "not to accommodate the effect of *shock*" (Ramos and Torres, 2005); and *ii*) when the source of inflationary pressures is of the other character, it is suggested to accommodate the

---

[15]These authors determine the above through the use of a vector autoregressive (VAR) model to characterize the shocks experienced by the Mexican economy during the three periods. VAR estimation allowed identifying the type of structural shocks affecting the product and prices.

shock to prevent the effect from falling "once for all" on the level of prices (first round effects).[16]

However, if this temporary effect on prices contaminated inflation expectations, then second-round price effects are recorded. In this situation, central bankers must modify the stance of monetary policy until expectations are once again aligned with the inflation targeting. It acknowledges that if the central bank follows these two requirements, the probability that monetary policy is an effective nominal anchor for the economy is significantly enhanced.

If central banks remain systematic, there are two recommendations that will significantly increase the likelihood that monetary policy (in this case, again we should refer to the nominal instrument of monetary policy) is an effective nominal anchor. Ramos and Torres (2005), however, propose that it is important to first identify inflationary pressures and secondly analyze the contribution of shocks (for they are those who must "accommodate"); usually, this type of shock is presented in the form of technological innovations, cyclic events of demand, and product prices.[17] The result presented by these authors is that there are no long-term effects on the product of demand shocks. The BANXICO technology shocks do not cause inflationary pressures.[18]

Summarizing the results obtained by Ramos and Torres (2005), the rigidity of the monetary policy during the three episodes revised was consistent with IT. In addition, they identified that the inflationary pressures of the first period came from the supply side in the form of "adverse shocks of costs." During the second episode, the expansion of aggregate demand was the cause of the pressures on inflation. And, in the last period, unwanted cost events again impacted on inflation. These are the reasons why the BANXICO restricted its stance of monetary policy.

Formalizing this, consistency of monetary policy with the principles of IT can be reviewed through a monetary policy rule as follows:

---

[16]Ramos-France and Torres, as an important part of the field responsible for the investigation of the Mexican central bank, say that there is some consensus in the literature of inflation targeting and the results are based on authors who have taken the reins of monetary policy of their respective countries; I am referring to Bernanke (1999) and Svensson (1997, 2000), in addition to Clarida (1999).

[17]The measurement of the effects of shocks takes place through a VAR structural model with monthly data specified in Ramos-France and Torres (2005), where the variable y_t is the product based on the IGAE and p_t INPC-based prices; they were analyzed by the Dickey–Fuller and Phillips–Perron unit-root tests. The result suggests that both variables are of order of integration of one

[18]Types of shocks to which reference is made present the characteristic of affecting prices "once for all" and affecting the product temporarily. This is useful for the identification of structural shocks.

$$i_t^* = \beta_0 + \beta_1 \pi_t^* + \beta_2 \left(\pi_{t+12}^e - \pi_{t+12}^* \right) + \beta_3 (y_t - y_t^*), \qquad (5.11)$$

where

i_t^* : is the desired interest rate,

π_t^* : is the target of annual inflation,

$\pi_{t+12}^e - \pi_{t+12}^*$: is the difference between expected annual inflation for 12 months and the 12-month target of annual inflation (inflation expectations gap), and

$y_t - y_t^*$: is the output gap.

Ramos and Torres (2005)-based analysis was carried out by Clarida et al. (1999), in which it is concluded that if the β_2- and β_3-rule (equation 5.11) coefficients are positive, then the rule is consistent with inflation targeting and, in the long term, induces inflation to converge to its target and the zero output gaps. Rule recommends increasing the real interest rate when you post a positive demand *shock* and both gaps increase. However, when inflationary pressures come from factors of cost, the recommendation is in general, not to adjust the interest rate. But if inflation expectations are affected by the *shock*, the increase in the gap of expectations of inflation will not compensate fully for the reduction of the output gap. When this happens, it is proposed to increase the interest rate to avoid second-round price effects.

Now, to determine whether monetary policy in Mexico has been consistent with the principles of the IT, specified in equation (5.11) rule, β_1 and β_2 parameters are evaluated statistically to be greater than one and zero, respectively. It is necessary to assume that interest rate i_t is determined as a weighted average of the desired interest rate i_t^* and the current interest rate observed in the previous period (i_{t-1}), more exogenous shock of the interest rate (v_t), with the characteristic that has mean zero:

$$i_t = (1 - \rho) i_t^* + \rho i_{t-1} + v_t. \qquad (5.12)$$

In this equation, the parameter ρ takes values from zero to one and measures the degree of "smoothing." Combining the required interest rate equation (5.11) with the smoothing equation (5.12) , the relationship to estimate is as follows:

$$i_t = (1-\rho)(\beta_0 + \beta_1\pi_t^* + \beta_2(\pi_{t+12}^e - \pi_{t+12}^*) + \beta_3(y_t - y_t^*)) + \rho i_{t-1} + v_t, \quad (5.13)$$

where

i_t : is a monthly average of the daily interbank interest rate,

π_t^* : is the target of annual inflation,

π_t^e : represents future 12-month annual inflation expectations, and

$y_t - y_t^*$: is the output gap.

Ramos and Torres (2005) document evidence that the process by which interest rates have been determined in Mexico is consistent with the approach of inflation targeting. The estimation of equation (5.13) shows that the coefficient of the inflation gap is statistically greater than one and the coefficient of the output gap is not statistically different from zero (or is zero). This suggests that for the period 1998-2003, "the process by which interest rates were formed implies that while inflation expectations grew, nominal and real interest rates were also growing" (Ramos and Torres, 2005). This means that the monetary policy rule anchored inflation expectations and inflation at its target.[19]

5.2   MINUTES AND REACTION FUNCTION

John Taylor encountered Robert Hetzel,[20] a critic who detected in the work of the first controversies that are worth reviewing. The first one is the one that refers to the concept of "observational equivalence," which basically implies that the Taylor rule conforms to the period that he uses, and therefore results will not agree to use another frequency. The second is that

---

[19]It is possible to extend the monetary policy rule explicitly by including the exchange rate, as shown below: $i_t^* = \beta_0 + \beta_1\pi_t^* + \beta_2(\pi_{t+12}^e - \pi_{t+12}^*) + \beta_2(y_t - y_t^*) + \beta_4 \Delta s_{t-1}$, where Δs_{t-1} represents the difference in log the monthly nominal exchange rate lagged in one period (pesos per dollar).

[20]He is a Senior Economist and Policy Advisor in the Research Department of the Federal Reserve Bank of Richmond, where he has served for over 30 years. The investigation of Hetzel has appeared in publications such as The *Journal of Money*, The *Journal of Monetary Economics,* in series of economic studies of the Bank of Japan, and in the lecture series at The Carnegie–Rochester conference.

in which Hetzel aims to point out the so-called "curve of Taylor," even though this is one of variability's breaks with the classical dichotomy that a nominal variable cannot affect a real variable, that is, it could only affect another nominal variable. Taylor responds to the above as seen in later paragraphs.

Hetzel reviewed the minutes from the Federal Reserve System (FED) and, from these, could deduce and pose a rule for monetary policy, which presents characteristics precisely discussed during the sessions of the FED. Hence it is that Hetzel doubted the veracity of the rule proposed by Taylor in 1993 and the problem of "observational equivalence." Therefore, this research will replicate what has been done by Hetzel at the FED with a considerable number of minutes to carry out its proposal for a monetary policy rule and, with it, try to determine the way it operates the US central bank (systematic component).

The replication will be held by a not-so-vast number of minutes from the BANXICO and intends to extract a systematic behavior of the interior of Mexico's monetary policy. Otherwise, you will reach the conclusion that the BANXICO does not follow any systematic behavior and, therefore, it is not, or it will not be possible to establish a rule for monetary policy for Mexico. In addition, one will say that the behavior of the issuing institution is one whose main characteristic is to act according to the context of the situation or the origin of inflationary pressures. We then proceed with this exercise.

It is important to begin with a timely description of the first minutes that was held in the BANXICO, as it was a relevant event that reinforces the strategy of communication of IT. Considering this, the first minutes in Mexico was conducted at 5 de Mayo Street, Number 2, 5th Floor, Colonia Centro, Mexico City, Federal District, which is home to the Mexican central bank. It is emphasized that it had preliminarily analyzed the economic and financial environment and particularly the behavior of inflation, its determinants, and their prospects.

The date on which the above-mentioned minute was recorded was January 20, 2011 and the attendees were Dr. Guillermo Carstens (Governor and President of the session), Lic. Roberto del Cueto Legaspi (Deputy Governor), Dr. Manuel Sánchez González (Deputy Governor), Dr. José Julián Sidaoui Dib (Deputy Governor), Act. Ernesto Javier Cordero Arroyo (Secretary of Finance and Public Credit), Maestro Gerardo Rodríguez Regordosa (Undersecretary of Finance and Public Credit), and Lic. Héctor Reynaldo Tinoco Jaramillo (Secretary of the Governing Board). All of the above is found in point number one of the minutes.

Following are the two points responsible for the recent economic and financial developments and prospects, which was prepared by the Directorate General of Economic Research and Operations of the Central Bank of the BANXICO. It starts with the analysis of the international economy, in which the minutes of the BANXICO begin with a good international environment, where global growth prospects for the year 2011 had improved.

The aforementioned recovery is generally for advanced economies, with the exception of Japan, and emerging economies with a strong and continuous growth. "In the first, the effect of the fiscal and monetary stimulus largely explains this improvement" (Banco de México, 2011a). For the USA, again, the growth forecasts had been revised upward due to monetary and fiscal stimuli. In Europe, Germany shows the largest gross domestic product (GDP) growth by far, despite persisting tension in financial markets, due to the economic performance of countries such as Portugal, Spain, and Belgium and their ability to meet financial needs.

This is related to an increase in the price of primary products due to an increase in demand and a reduction in supply worldwide. Some emerging economies, particularly China, tried to stop the increase in inflation through monetary restrictive measures, increasing the reference rates and commercial bank reserve requirements, and they tracked actions (including price controls). Subsequently, the Bill includes financial evolution of developed markets, emerging markets, and the Mexican market. Highlights of the first stock indexes advanced favorably since 2010, which means more investor risk aversion.

In addition, there was a depreciation of the euro against major currencies due to the fiscal and financial situation of some European countries. What is relevant in emerging countries is that due to the presence of liquidity in the world then, the emerging economies offered them more attractive yields and therefore, investors directed their resources to such countries. However, and as is persistent in emerging countries, there is concern regarding the speed and magnitude of these capital flows.[21]

It is suggested that the behavior of the average of the economies of emerging countries should combat inflationary pressures by increasing interest rates. However, this will cause an increase in the attractiveness for the entry of capital flows. Faced with this dilemma, several countries have resorted to interventions in the foreign exchange market[22] or to "adopt prudential macromeasures mainly to raise the requirements of reserves of the banking institutions" (Banco de México, 2011a). The Bill emphasizes that the expectation that in major developed countries, short-term interest rates remain at very low levels injected certainty in financial markets.

In the case of the Mexican markets, as it is called in the minutes, it is said that at the end of 2010, a currency appreciation process derived from various sources was conducted: *i*) the favorable impact of the best expectations of growth of the USA, *ii*) hiring by Mexico's line of credit with the IMF, and *iii*) high oil prices. Once posed, this continues with economic activity and inflation in Mexico. With regard to the first, Mexican production showed a positive trend during the last quarter of 2010. The above was derived from favorable behaviors of both external and internal demands.

In what refers to the determinants of inflation, the minutes participant number one considered that the evolution of aggregate demand (positive) results showed that the output gap will be reduced. In addition, the external account deficit is moderate, which is reflected in the absence of pressure. Similarly, considerable amounts of resources from abroad contributed to settlement of current account *deficits*, causing at the same time an appreciation of the local currency and a significant increase in international reserves.

In addition, it was anticipated that the output gap would be closed during 2011. It was recognized that if the inflation gap became positive at some point, it would be caused by pressure in the main markets of inputs. Thus, the expectations of inflation by the end of 2011 remained stable

---

[21]Workflows can cause "appreciation of currencies in countries" with regimes of flexible exchange rate and its possible impact on the competitiveness of its exports, the excessive expansion of credit, and the possible formation of "bubbles" in asset prices, as well as the possibility that the volume of foreign capital inflows can leave the economies vulnerable to sudden departures of such flows, (Banco de México, 2011. This is the first minute).

[22]This (intervention in the foreign exchange market) evidence was established in the chapter room, but Calvo and Reinhart raised the fear of floating and obviously breaks with the theory proposed by John Taylor to achieve a good monetary policy, i.e., with the Taylor *tripod*.

(around 3.8%). Also, it is recognized that long-term inflation expectations have remained anchored at levels above 3%.

In Mexico, in the context of the evolution and prospects for inflation (according to the minute number one), annual headline inflation stood at 4.4% by the end of 2010 and, according to the minutes number one, the evolution of the overall inflation was congruent with that proposed by the issuing institution. This obviously is outside the range of 3% ±1% of variability; however, the participating signatories of the present minutes considered it is consistent because of the subprime (financial) and economic crises in recent years.

For the signatories of the first minutes in Mexico, no underlying component generated the largest increase observed in the general rate of inflation and the underlying remained almost constant. The factors that contributed to the situation that no underlying component will generate pressures was attributed to the following: *i*) exchange rate parity, *ii*) negative levels of product, *iii*) moderate wage revisions, and *iv*) increased competition in the commercial sector gap.

However, the effects of the above factors were eliminated by the rises in the prices of certain foods, especially those related to corn and wheat. The BANXICO and the Secretary of Finance and Public Credit, through their owners, provided for not only that the annual headline inflation for 2011 would descend, but also that they converge to their target of 3% in mid-2011, the percentage above and below the target point. In addition to the above, the behavior of inflation in Mexico could face, says the Bill, several potential risks that attend *i*) a further lifting of international prices of grains, *ii*) price of goods and services defined by local governments, *iii*) the behavior of the output gap, and *iv*) exchange rate volatility.

Advancing in the minutes, the members of the Governing Board conduct an analysis and pose some of their reasons for their votes, which are consistent with all of the issues raised so far by the minutes. It is relevant and important to clarify that the minutes in Mexico still have not developed fully; this is because the approaches and individual interventions of the participants are registered anonymously. In my opinion, this is a trait that detracts from the strategy of communication and accountability, which the BANXICO has aligned itself with a focus on inflation targeting.

Once the above is clarified, it is recorded by the participants that the vulnerability of the international financial system is a factor that limits global economic growth in the medium term. There is also the concern of one of the signatories of the minutes that the situation of some countries of the European Union (EU) is worsening and that "the observed recovery of developed economies will weaken when monetary and fiscal stimuli are no longer sustainable and interest rates will be pressed to boost" (Banco de México, 2011a).

Concerning the output gap, it argues that it could be possible for 2011 to be on positive ground, but there are factors limiting the potential, e.g., *i*) installed capacity is lower than the precrisis levels, *ii*) the rate of unemployment is considerably high, and *iii*) wage increases have been moderate. It should be noted that all members of the Board agreed that the evolution of inflation was good during 2010 due to factors such as *i*) the level of the output gap, *ii*) appreciation of the currency, *iii*) labor market slack, and *iv*) inflation expectations remained well anchored. The style of the minutes takes us into descriptions of this type: "some" members of the Board noted that deviations from general inflation with respect to target expectations were essentially due to no underlying component, "which certainly may be affected by monetary policy in a very small way" (Banco de México, 2011a). At the same time, the Bill cites that "all" members of the Board noted that the "better prospects for the Mexican economy and the environment of abundant liquidity at the international level have been reflected in considerable inputs of capital flows" and that "the fact that an important part of these flows is directed to debt instruments is a reflection of the confidence of investors in the anchoring of inflation expectations" (Banco de México, 2011a).

Once again "a" member of the Board establishes additional factors underpinning forecast that the inflation would continue falling in 2011: *i*) the elimination of the effect of tax measures and adjustments to public rates in 2010, and *ii*) lower prices for tourist services, among others, including the stance of monetary policy consistent with the convergence of inflation to the target of 3% and the competition between retail chains. Finally, the Board members and signatories of the first minutes made by the central bank of the country came to the next monetary policy decision.

The Government Board of the BANXICO decided to keep 4.5% as the target for the interbank interest rate overnight by unanimity. It is also recognized that to avoid unexpected pressures and character-generalized price, it is necessary to monitor the behavior of the expectations of inflation, output gap, and public prices, particularly the price of grains and other commodities. Thus, we can say that the BANXICO reacts to changes in the output gap, inflation, and expectations; to the exchange rate field; and structural and short-term factors that affect the price level.

So, it can be determined that reaction of the issuing Mexican institution is formed, as specified by equation (5.3) of Section 5.1 of this chapter and raised by Torres in 2002:

$$i_t = \alpha + \beta\left(E_t\left[\pi_{t+n} - \pi^*\right]\right) + \gamma\left(E_t\left[y_{t+k} - y_{t+k}^*\right]\right) + \varphi(E_t[z_{t+m}]), \quad (5.3)$$

where z_{t+m} : represents the set of variables that could possibly influence the stance of monetary policy.

Once the scenario was posed, the BANXICO issued in its first minutes of specified and monetary-policy decision a possible role of reaction (see equation 5.3), the evolution of the minutes follows. For this, you need to review the way in which we have been publishing, i.e., the format, points touched, issues raised, the intentions of the interventions, and the printed transparency level on the document. With regard to the latter, I mean essentially whether it is continuous writing in third person or the opinions of the participants of the meeting.

The second minutes of BANXICO were conducted 6 weeks later, i.e., on March 3, 2011, attended by the same participants of the Board of Government and by officials of the Ministry of Finance and Public Credit. It is immediately noticed that the central bank intended to emphasize the positions of participants, that is, pronouns such as "everyone," "the majority," a, another, etc., referring to the signatory participants of this second Bill, appear underlined. This emphasis was not present in the initial minutes, so it is relevant to highlight it since it represents the need for the Governing Board to show union and coordination in the monetary decision making.

Also, it should be noted that the main arguments of this second document are mostly resumed from the first minutes, since its behavior persists. Current account and trade balance deficits remained at moderate levels by the end of 2010, which suggests, according to the minutes, greater dynamism of exports with regard to the imports. Also this ensures that there is no demand on the formation of price pressures in the economy and persistent pressures on inflation expectations due to its inconsistent component.

Other factors to consider as determinants of inflation in Mexico for this period are lower growth of agricultural prices and greater competition among retail chains. However, there are increased risks to inflation due to the increase in raw materials, considered also in the review of the special tax on production and services to tobacco. "Other types of risks that could affect the inflation are perturbations of the costs due to the volatility of fuel prices and the volatility of the exchange rate" (Banco de México, 2011b). This is associated with the international geopolitical environment[23]; however, the Mexican issuing institution expected inflation to converge to its target.[24]

Finally, the monetary policy decision was to keep 4.5% a day as the target for the interbank interest rate unanimously and emphasized that monetary authorities should not react to variations (especially increases) of sustained relative prices. This is because the effects of monetary policy are only with lags, which means that they do not intervene immediately on these variations. This means that monetary policy has effects only in the medium to long term.

From the third minute set, a pattern emerges in terms of the frequency of occurrence of the same. This means, this happens every 6 weeks, which marks that the observance of such minutes will take place on April 14, 2011. A characteristic feature that immediately emerges is that the BANXI-CO uses "econometric exercises" to analyze the labor market; particularly the degree of wage increases during similar periods revised. The exercises consist of "estimated Phillips curves, where nominal wage increases are determined on the basis of the output gap, of the expectations of inflation, and remnants of the three previous variables" (Banco de México, 2011).

It also highlights that the current recovery of the economic activity of the country is largely due to the dynamics of exports, which has caused one of the lowest levels of current account deficit since the 1990s to be registered. Inflation expectations are anchored, although above the threshold of 3% because the appreciation of the local currency has acted as a counterweight to the increases in international prices of raw materials. Also, it argues that price reductions experienced by certain groups of agricultural products, and not the underlying component, have contributed to the reduction in inflation.

It announced a forecast for inflation, where the risk of turbulence in international financial markets could lead to reallocation of portfolios and

---

[23]These factors are, for example, the deleveraging of the families in the USA, the deterioration of the fiscal stance of the advanced economies, and the possible departure of a eurozone country.

[24]In addition, this shows the difficulty in historical calculation of the output gap since this is made by a nonobservable variable.

large capital flows that can cause exchange rate variability. This forecast envisages that annual headline inflation path is placed at higher probability of occurrence between 3% and 4%. The above stems from the position of members of the Governing Board with voting rights (the Governor and the Subgubernators of the BANXICO), which shows that there is confidence that during 2011 and 2012, inflation behaves according to schedule but that there are still risks to consider in general terms: *i*) the sustainability of the economic recovery worldwide, *ii*) the evolution of the exchange rate and of the prices of raw materials, and *iii*) the evolution of inflation expectations.[25]

In the first quarter of 2011, a decrease in inflation was expected and in March, its minimum. A member of the Board said that this was due to factors that will not be repeated, in particular, the reduction of the prices of some agricultural products. Also, a member of the Board said that it must monitor underlying inflation and that it converges to 3%. In addition, a member made a peculiar speech since he questions the ability of monetary policy to fight not underlying inflation, particularly the importance of identifying the nature of inflationary pressures mentioned herein and whether the intervention of the monetary authorities is the best and the only instrument.

It documented that the weakness in the housing market continues and the state of the international financial system. In addition, other members of the Board indicated that there is uncertainty about the evolution of the exchange rate in future, this means, in the bosom of the BANXICO is the fear of potential appreciation of the local currency, affecting inflation. The Board stressed that the policy of the Federal Government that isolates external pressures from domestic prices has contributed to mitigate the impact on inflation in Mexico.[26] In the end, the Governing Board of the BANXICO decided to keep 4.5% target for interbank interest rate unanimously.

Six weeks later, minutes number four was conducted in May 27, 2011, attended by the same participants with the proviso that the Deputy Governor of the BANXICO, Dr. Manuel Ramos Francia, join the signing of this document. One of the elements that I call to attention is that it is said that

---

[25]A Board member noted that within the conditions that determine inflation in Mexico is global inflation.

[26]However, another Board Member mentioned that the referred insulation is only temporary because if international oil prices remain at their current levels, then you have repressed inflation, which sooner or later is going to manifest itself.

"the level of the average income of the jobs that have been generated during the recovery of the economy is less than the jobs that were lost during the recessive phase" (Banco de México, 2011d). Furthermore, it is said for different horizons, inflation expectations remained anchored in the range of variability.

A Board member raised as additional risk the uncertainty of the sustainability of private spending in the USA, once the monetary and fiscal policy stimulus fades. The minutes said that prospects of slower economic growth and lower prices of raw materials have improved the inflation picture. However, pressures on inflation have been experienced, and the difference between actual inflation and the target inflation (inflation gap) in the majority of economies (advanced and emerging) is considerably lower than the levels that these indicators had achieved prior to the global financial crisis.

In addition, the major advanced economies will prevail over the accommodative monetary stance to deal with the situation of rise in the prices of raw materials, also showing a weakening of the country's economic recovery process. However, some Board members pointed out that the growth slowdown is temporary and due to unavailable indicators such as consumption, formal employment, and the increase in bank lending. At the same time, it was pointed out by a member that Mexico is the only country in a sample of 25 emerging economies where inflation is consistently above its goal since 2005. What makes evident the need for greater effectiveness in the anchoring of inflation at its target?

They acknowledged that the evolution of employment and salaries affects price formation and all the participants agreed that the behavior of the exchange had a role in the reduction of the inflation rate. In this way, limited exchange rate volatility, as well as its appreciation, contributed to the price of tradable inflation, which was reduced. It also noted that agricultural commodities prices contributed to the decline of inflation. Considering the above, the Government Board of the BANXICO decided to keep 4.5% as the target for the interbank interest rate overnight by unanimity.

Minutes number five were held on July 8, 2011 and it was attended by the same participants as at the previous meeting; i.e., it boasts the presence of Deputy Governor Dr. Manuel Ramos Francia. It should be noted that in the present minutes, reference to the "recent financial developments" point and the subtopic of "developed markets" was omitted. The main reality that the Board recognizes is that the pace of recovery in Mexico has moderated (since the prospects for global growth have been revised downward) and that, however, the reported levels of inflation are offspring experienced in the past 5 years, particularly the inflation in services.

During the first four minutes were mentioned previous risks, present and potential, but the minute number five refers to these as the "balance of risks." In this context, it was said that the balance of risks in the global economy has deteriorated and resulted, in my opinion, in the unconventional use of the median as the measure of central tendency to describe the slowdown of GDP forecasts for the rest of 2011.

An additional feature that I call attention to is this: a member of the Board said that the weakness of the global economy is deeper than what is said and that "expansionary policies are not sustainable" (Banco de México, 2011e). This is outstanding because at no previous time had such position been taken by a member of the Board.[27]

This shows that once again, Mexico is strongly influenced negatively by events in the neighboring countries of the North, such as the weakness of the labor market and housing. Also, Europe's problems could have a negative impact on the process of decision of monetary policy in Mexico. In particular, concerning Greece, Europe is having political difficulties in implementing austerity measures and the potential for contamination of Portugal, Ireland, and Spain. Regarding prices, the Board generally acknowledged that there are risks due to overheating of emerging economies and, therefore, their inflation is high.

In addition, all members said that the rise in raw material prices has begun to be reversed, thanks to products such as oil, corn, wheat, and some industrial metals. Another Board Member said that they did not perceive signs of pressure on inflation coming from wages in the advanced economies. For Mexico, the Board detected a minor internal dynamism resulting from low levels of consumer confidence and this could worsen due to the unfavorable conditions that prevail in the labor market (highly persistent unemployment rate). It is here that participants reiterated their confidence in an indicator, in particular, the IGAE, to determine, despite the interruption of the Mexican recovery, the growth forecast of the country for 2011 and 2012.

The signatories of the minutes argue that due to low levels of inflation in recent years, particularly services inflation, "the current monetary stance of the BANXICO has been and remains correct" (Banco de México,

---

[27]In addition, this is intended for the case of the European Union restrictions on fiscal policies.

2011e). This allowed that expectations and forecasts of inflation is adjusted downward, which knit inflation to its target. A member asked for caution regarding the good behavior of inflation since it could follow a lasting deviation from the target, prices of agricultural goods will likely return to increased values, and finally, some public prices would become constant.

Finally, please note that only if the economic conditions become even more unfavorable in Europe, the foreign exchange category could mean a risk for inflation. And, it concludes with the statement that the balance of risks to inflation in Mexico has improved. The decision of monetary policy for this Bill was "keep 4.5% goal for the interbank interest rate a day." This decision was adopted by unanimity.

On August 26, 2011 was held the minutes number 6, with the presence of the same members as in that preceding this meeting, with the exception of Act. Ernesto Cordero Arroyo. Again the subitem relating to "recent financial evolution in developed countries" was omitted. Thus, the Board established that the balance of risks to the growth of the Mexican economy has deteriorated, while the balance of inflation risks had improved. In general terms, the six meetings of minutes take up the issues raised in the previous one, since in the USA, fiscal problems persist and the sovereign crisis continues in several European countries; moreover, global financial instability was accentuated at the end of July.

This last resulted in the price of gold, the Swiss franc, and yen to appreciate against the dollar, which caused their central banks to relax their monetary policies. However, this period also recorded the appreciation phenomenon of the US dollar with respect to the currencies of emerging countries. With respect to the national economy, the perceptions of growth are good, although a Board Member warned that there might be some seasonal effect and that, despite the location of the USA, exports would dwindle. Also, the majority of the members of the Board established a process of narrowing the gap of continuous product and highlighted encouraging indicators such as the level of debt, since they are, in relative terms, the lowest in the world and there it helps to achieve the convergence of inflation targeting congruence between fiscal and monetary policies.

It is considered that the international prices of oil and the domestic gap have helped contain inflation despite the fiscal cost associated with it. In this review, there were increases in prices of food, beverages, and tobacco, which can negatively affect the formation of expectations of private agents. A process of rising cost of services due to the prevailing insecurity in the country is suggested. Thus, long-term inflation expectations are not approaching the permanent target and the short remains at ceiling level. This implies that deviations from the target could increase with an environment of greater uncertainty.

However, "some members of the Board noted that there is an inflation risk derived from a more complex economic environment, insisting that the type of change, which has been a favorable factor in the evolution of inflation, could be reversed in the future" (Banco de México, 2011f). Due to the persistent differential between Mexico and US interest rates, it could tighten the monetary policy of Mexico; however, there is a risk of increase in uncertainty by sending a lack of commitment of monetary authorities to achieve the permanent target.

In this regard, a member of the Board stressed that the work of the Bank is to meet the inflation targeting at the lowest possible cost to society and that having a more restrictive position as the circumstances merit would generate costs that would be desirable to avoid. Finally, the decision of monetary policy by the Government Board of the BANXICO was to keep on 4.5% as the target for the interbank interest rate a day. This decision was taken by unanimity. They claim that given the conditions of the national economy and international financial markets, increase in the restrictive monetary policy sounds unnecessary.

The minute number seven was held on October 14, 2011 and it highlights the absence of Act. Ernesto Cordero Arroyo, due to his resignation to seek the nomination of the national action party for the Presidency of the Republic. Instead the Secretary of Finance and Public Credit, Dr. José Antonio Meade Kuribreña, assumes the post and, therefore, attends the review of monetary policy with members of the Governing Board who regularly sign the BANXICO minutes. It persists in the omission of the subitem relating to "recent financial evolution in developed countries."

It is designated as the main axis that has weakened the global economic activity and an increase in the volatility of the financial markets. He stressed that since the previous minutes had expressed that provided a favorable behavior of international economic activity, we simply had to take into consideration some potential risks. Therefore, the Governing Board declares that the balance of risks to the growth of the Mexican economy had deteriorated, while the respective inflation had registered an improvement. It is necessary to show that a (small) part of the Board considers that the balance of risks to inflation did not improve, i.e., it has been affected negatively.

The reasons why the Board considered that the balance risks of the product had deteriorated were as follows: *i*) problems of fiscal sustainability and the crisis of sovereign debt in Europe,[28] EU, and other advanced economies, *ii*) one member stressed that the credit around the world could experience reductions, and *iii*) another Member stated that pessimism has been assumed even though the monetary stance has been very lax for many years and there has been a clear positive effect. In addition, risks of the US economy, such as weakening of the job market, mortgage, and household debt problems, should be incorporated. All of this leads to a possible reduction in private consumption.

All of the above has caused volatility in the exchange rates (depreciation of most currencies against the dollar), falls in generalized container values, and increases in interest rates. This is quoted separately from the components of the balance of risks by the BANXICO, which stands out in the minutes number seven, since they had been considered as such (parts of the balance of risks) in the previous minutes. This means that the Mexican issuing institution has stopped considering them as risks to be assumed as the effects of international financial turbulence. Therefore, one could say that the BANXICO has amended its reaction function, this means, it responds to other variables or indicators.

The possibility arises for the first time that in a Bill is presented a catastrophic event (even remote) that is unequivocal sign of nervousness in the financial markets, by what is proposed as the crucial intervention of advanced countries to anchor inflation expectations and thus eliminate the probability of a catastrophic event. "In this way, it would solve the problem of financial turbulence and the global economy would then be located in a situation of a deceleration, with which the markets know to deal in an orderly manner" (Banco de México, 2011g). Therefore, if expectations stabilize through credible commitments, obviously there will not be fiscal balance and full employment, but it would be an orderly notorious adjustment.

In Mexico, according to the Board, the depreciation of the peso against the dollar has had no significant impact on inflation or expectations. This means that the BANXICO consistently monitors the behavior of the ex-

---

[28]Some members of the Board considered that this deterioration and the lack of credible, sufficient, and satisfactory actions have been causal for the relevant international financial turbulence that exists today.

change rate and, therefore, we can say that it reacts to that variable. Additionally, it was said that the price of some commodities like maize will serve as an additional element for the stability of inflation. However, a Board Member said that the balance of risk of inflation for Mexico has deteriorated and that stable behavior is based on factors that are not sustainable. Finally, it was decided to keep on 4.5% as the target for the interbank interest rate a day. This decision was adopted by unanimity.

A cut here, right in the seventh minutes from the BANXICO, to establish in a preliminary way the proposal of function of reaction of the Mexican issuing institution, which this document seeks to make, is made. This effort is structuring a systematic real component that is based on the decisions of monetary policy of the Government Board of the BANXICO and that, so far, is suggested as follows:

$$i_t = \alpha + \beta\left(E_t\left[\pi_{t+n} - \pi^*\right]\right) + \varphi(E_t[z_{t+m}]), \qquad (5.3b)$$

where z_{t+m}: represents the set of variables that could possibly influence the stance of monetary policy.

You can see that the suggestion of rule of policy established by this research does not consider the output gap due to the nature of the rule of law on BANXICO, i.e., unique mandate. However, it remains a component that collects the set of variables that affect the monetary policy decision. Again, there was an intense, constant, and concerned interest for the monitoring of the exchange rate variable. It is for this reason that the component

of the rule z_{t+m}, serving as a detector of exchange rate variability, prevails. Thus, we continue with the realization of the searching function of reaction of the Mexican Monetary Institute with a slogan to make it still more specific.

On December 2, 2011, the Board of BANXICO Government held the eighth minutes for the determination of the monetary policy decision. Maestro Gerardo Rodríguez Regordosa is absent and instead Dr. José Antonio González Anaya, Undersecretary of Income of the Secretaría de Hacienda y Crédito Público, joins. This Bill emphasizes that some members of the Board consider that the balance of risks to inflation in Mexico is no longer favorable to be "neutral" and growth has worsened. This meant that it considered the possibility of a catastrophic event, with the inherent consequences such as the deterioration of the financial situation and economic growth, even more likely.

Paradoxically, for the first time in several months, growth forecasts for the USA were revised upward; however, these expectations were marginal. In general, problems persist in the USA and Europe with the same implications for Mexico. The Federal Reserve Bank was found in relative tranquility since it did not worry about inflationary pressures. Therefore, the institution emphasized that its stance of monetary policy will remain loose at least until mid-2013. Also, some members of the Board stated that "there is concern in several emerging countries that there is an effect of the depreciation of the exchange about the inflation rates" (Banco de México, 2011h).

Contrary to what has been proposed, a member of the Board argued that growth prospects improved moderately despite the European situation and that expectation of economic growth for the USA that directly affect Mexico improved. Also, "the majority of the members of the Board said that moderate inflation observed during 2011 responded inter alia to the fact that the output gap continued to be negative" (Banco de México, 2011h). The above shows that if the observed product is not greater than the potential product, then inflationary pressures will be minimal.

In addition to the product, according to BANXICO gap, inflation has remained stable due to large slack in the labor market, the exchange rate in the first part of the year, levels of public insecurity in some parts of the country, greater competition in some sectors, a very important negative change of the index of fruits and vegetables, and the subsidy of the price of energy. The former chief, for the purposes of this paper, a member of the staff of the central institution, recognized that only exchange rate influences inflation in a part of the year, which means that the Mexico Bank reaction function undergoes changes, although marginal, during the management of monetary policy.

However, it was added in the minutes that permanence of a high exchange rate could bring negative impact on price formation and contaminating inflation expectations in the medium and long terms, as well as back unsustainable subsidies to energy. To combat this, a participant said in the minutes that reserve accumulation and a flexible credit line for the stabilization of the rate of change and expectations are necessary. Finally, it highlights that the possible elements that would affect the inflation are droughts and commodity prices. Once all of the above are considered, it was decided to hold 4.5% as the target for the interbank overnight rate, as in all the previous minutes, interest rate was rendered unmoving.

The new minutes were conducted on January 20, 2012 and for the minutes, far greater presence was recorded as nine officials of the BANXICO and the Secretaría de Hacienda y Crédito Público were present: Dr. Agustín Guillermo Carstens (Governor and President of the session), Lic. Roberto of the Legaspi Cueto (Deputy Governor), Dr. Manuel Ramos Francia (Deputy Governor), Dr. Manuel Sánchez González (Deputy Governor), Dr. José Julián Sidaoui Dib (Deputy Governor), Dr. José Antonio Meade Kuribreña (Secretary of Finance and Public Credit), Maestro Gerardo Rodríguez Regordosa (Undersecretary of Finance and Public Credit), Dr. José Antonio González Anaya (Undersecretary of Income of the Secretaría de Hacienda y Crédito Público), and Lic. Héctor Reynaldo Tinoco Jaramillo (Secretary of the Junta of Gobierno).

Far early in the year and, therefore, for this minute, it is shown that the probability of a catastrophic event happening is decreased. However, the balance of risks to growth in Mexico continued to deteriorate and the corresponding inflation remained stable. For the Board, economic activity in Mexico continues its expansion although it now does so at lower rates; an item that caught my attention is that a Member said that US growth is not expected to give a considerable stimulus in the following years. As for inflation, the Board said "the recent increase in headline inflation was mainly due to an increase in noncore inflation, to which a Member said that the increase is marginal and that it is due to temporary factors that do not seem to have had side effects of relevance" (Banco de México, 2012a).

The conclusion of the minutes number ten with the same members of the Board of the earlier session gathered on March 15, 2012. With respect to the balance of risks to inflation, the Board said that it has improved. The Governing Board agreed that given global conditions of growth and inflation expectations, it is expected that major central banks of the world act with accommodative monetary posture. The more relevant point is that "the United States Federal Reserve has ratified its decision to keep the great monetary lassitude and all of its nonconventional forward policies even until 2014" (Banco de México, 2012b).

To the Board, the Mexican economy continues to expand and it is resistant to various shocks from abroad. Also other key indicators that showed positive behavior in the manufacturing and industrial sector were stressed. It is considered that from the previous minutes, the Governing Board began to worry about the seasonal component, essentially by the increase in consumption resulting from the festivities of December that passed on the credit and an increase in formal employment and a member said that it is foreseeable that the Mexican economy is approaching its growth potential in an orderly manner over the next few years. This, in my opinion, is a little sustained and therefore risky argument.

The Board considered that the appreciation of the peso against the dollar at the beginning of 2012 and the best position of sovereign risk has increased significantly, so the trend of holdings of Government securities held by foreigners increased, demonstrating the greater confidence of the country for investors. As for inflation, the levels of public insecurity have influenced the inflation in services; however, the Board agreed that inflation expectations are well anchored and argued that, in the short term, these had suffered mild impairment and warned some pressure as being close: food prices, weather phenomena, and the volatility of international markets.

Some members said that the good behavior of the inflation is due essentially to the credibility of the Mexican issuing institution in reaching its target with appropriate messages and recognizing that the main channel of transmission is precisely the instrument of monetary policy used by the BANXICO. A member of the Board, with whom I agree, said that if you judge by the underlying inflation, the inflation targeting already would have reached. Therefore, the Government Board of the BANXICO, whereas interventions made by members and invited officials from the Ministry of finance and public credit, decided to keep on 4.5% the target for the interbank interest rate a day. This decision was adopted by unanimity.

On April 27, 2012 took place minutes number eleven, it was signed by the same people from the previous session, with the absences of José Antonio Meade Kuribreña, Gerardo Rodríguez Regordosa, and José Antonio González Anaya, who agreed that the balance of risks to inflation has remained unchanged and that monetary policy will remain accommodative in almost all economies, in particular, the Federal Reserve has decided to maintain its extremely lax monetary policy stance. It emphasized that the output gap had been closing gradually; however, the labor slack caused pressures on inflation. The above dismisses any possibility that the country reaches a level of unemployment that accelerates inflation.

It continues to hold that inflation expectations are well anchored and general and underlying inflation will be consistent with those of the

BANXICO for 2012 and 2013. However, a member of the Board said that he saw no way by which inflation is approaching its target for any term. Also from the inflationary pressures of agricultural products, food prices are recognized; the latter is worrying due to potential contamination of the price formation process. The exchange rate then suffered a rise, this means, weight against the dollar is compared, but so far, this behavior is, to the Board, stable and well behaved.

This Bill agrees that monetary policy in México does not guarantee that inflation converges to its target and that it has not achieved this due to "transitory shocks in relative prices" (Banco de México, 2012c). Finally, the Board decided to keep 4.5% as the target for the interbank interest rate unanimously. There is a monetary policy stance of monitoring of developed and emerging countries (LAX) as this could be an indication that Mexican monetary authorities will step to a relaxation. And, at all times, it seeks to reach the convergence of inflation to the permanent target of 3%.

The penultimate session was held on 8 June this year, i.e., the twelfth (so far) minutes of decision of monetary policy in Mexico, which was attended and signed by the same members of the previous minutes. The Board said that the balance of risks to inflation remains constant, with risks of worsening. There is consensus that "inflation expectations remain anchored and clearly below 4%" (Banco de México, 2012d). Regarding risks to the rise in inflation, the Board drew the conclusion that a mild effect of transfer of the inflation rate has been noted. However, it warned that if this situation (the depreciated peso) continues, pressures and the effects of change on inflation will begin to be considered dangerous or harmful.

Another source of pressure on inflation is the price of energy and food prices. It agreed that type change impacts have existed, these were mild and transient, and therefore, there is no evidence of the presence of second-order effects. It also stressed the role played by the stance of monetary policy as a factor in containment of inflation, in particular, it has maintained a reduced transfer of the movements of exchange on prices and has made it possible for the real exchange rate to function as an efficient absorber of external shocks. Finally, the Board retained 4.5% as its instrument of monetary policy again.

Finally, regarding the review of minutes of July 20, 2012, the last minutes that will enter into the analysis and proposition of a function of reaction from the BANXICO was held. Members of the Board who signed it are Agustín Guillermo Carstens Carstens, as Governor and President of the session, Roberto del Cueto Legaspi, Manuel Ramos Francia, Manuel

Sánchez González, and Héctor Reynaldo Tinoco. Risks to inflation, which could result in pressures, such as the price of agricultural products and the recent outbreak of influenza detected in birds, and the global slowdown have given clearance on commodity prices. It is for this reason that emphasis was placed on improving the mechanisms of communication to the public.

It is necessary to note that, during the period of analysis, all members of the Board of Governors made considerations concerning the behavior of the exchange rate. It was pointed out that there has been a trend toward the real depreciation of the peso against the dollar; however, the efforts of the macroeconomics in reacting to external shocks have been adequate, spearheaded by "a prudent fiscal stance and a monetary policy conducive to the convergence of inflation" (Banco de México, 2012e). This has allowed the real depreciation of the peso to be specified in an orderly manner and with a minimum transfer of the nominal parity adjustment of prices to the final consumer. Finally, the Board decided to keep unchanged the instrument of monetary policy.

The scenario posed by the 13 minutes held by the BANXICO as an effort to reinforce transparency and accountability, fundamental aspects of IT, allows one to set the conditions necessary to propose or suggest a "new" reaction to the function of the Mexican issuing institution. Thus, whereas the mandates of the Mexican central institute and the Governing Board identify how all pressures on inflation, such as the price of food, agricultural products, etc., are transient, emphasizing that the behavior of the issuing institute is characterized by action according to the situation or the origin of inflationary pressures.

The previous review shows that a possible role of reaction that emanates from the minutes of the Government Board of the BANXICO is as follows:

$$i_t = \alpha + \beta \left(E_t \left[\pi_{t+n} - \pi^* \right] \right) + \gamma (E_t[e_o - e^R]), \qquad (5.3c)$$

where

α is the equilibrium real interest rate over the long term,

π_{t+n}: is the inflation between period t and the period $t + n$,

π^* : is the permanent target of inflation of 3%,

e_o : is the observed exchange rate,

e^R : is the representative exchange rate, and

E_t : is the operator's expectations that form with the information available in the period t.

For the estimation of this policy rule that was derived from the analysis of the minutes of the BANXICO monetary policy decision and, therefore, for the 2008 period: 01 to 2012:03, we used the following series. For π_{t+n}, the annualized inflation rate. For e_o, the type of change in pesos per dollar to settle liabilities denominated in foreign currency.[29] And the representative change e^R, the median derived using the Hodrick–Prescott filter.[30] The operator of expectations is used in the reaction function simply to specify that it is a function that looks forward (*forward looking*). Below are the results of the estimation:

$$ i_t = 4.16 + 1.18\left(\pi_{t+n} - \pi_t^*\right) - 0.53\left(e_o - e^R\right) + u_t, \qquad (5.14) $$

S.D.: (0.29) (0.17) (0.17),
Prob.: [0.0000] [0.0000] [0.0042],
$R^2 = 0.49$
Durbin–Watson statistic (DW) = 0.22

The estimate reveals a coefficient for the top one inflation gap, indicating that BANXICO intends to act in some way similar to that proposed in the beginning by Taylor. In addition, it should be noted that the probability associated with this coefficient is less than 0.05, which shows that we are in the presence of a statistically significant parameter. For its part, the exchange rate gap coefficient turned out to be negative, however significant. The interpretation of this is that for variations of 1% in the exchange rate gap, the instrument of monetary policy (nominal interest rate) must be adjusted –0.53 times. It is also evident that the estimation of the reaction function proposed is autocorrelation since the DW statistic is 0.22 and confirmed using the Breusch–Godfrey test of serial correlation.

---

[29]We used this type of change in particular since the series is monthly.
[30]This was true since obtaining the type of representative change by another method, for example, by obtaining moving averages implies a considerable loss of information. This was so, because a moving average represents a tendency of the variable of interest, therefore, the use of the Hodrick–Prescott filter has the same effect, with the exception of not allowing the loss of elements of the series, making inference of estimates more significant.

The inclusion of the exchange rate variable in the reaction function proposed is somewhat complicated, considering the formulation of monetary policy, since it is not enough to unlink the movements of the exchange rate from the domestic interest rate with capital controls and the interventions of sterilization. Thus, the question of Taylor (2001) is how should instruments of monetary policy react to exchange rate movements? Alternatively, central bankers must avoid any reaction and focus on domestic indicators (inflation and product). Taylor did not linked his rule of 1993 to the exchange rate since the simulations of the model on which it was based showed that if a central bank reacts strongly to the exchange rate variable, then the macroeconomic performance would be worse. However, this conclusion is not clear for other countries, especially for the developing ones.

In the case of equation (5.14), e_o increase implies a real appreciation of the local currency. Given the above and in the context of the equation that we are concerned, the question about the role of the type of change in a monetary rule focuses on the characteristics of the parameter of the exchange rate gap.[31] Since we are talking about the Mexican economy, it may be that the coefficient of the exchange rate gap is different from zero (as is the case); however, such terminology might be very misleading because in reality, the optimal policy for an open economy is one that defines the coefficient of the variable exchange rate as zero, at least as an approximation. Then, if the exchange rate gap parameter is nonzero, what sign should it be?

A possible interpretation is that proposed by Obstfeld and Rogoff (1995), who say that if the exchange rate gap coefficient is less than zero, then a higher-than-"normal" real exchange rate implies that the issuing institution should reduce the short-term interest rate, "which presumably could represent a relaxation of monetary policy" (Taylor, 2001). To support the above, I will refer to the issues raised by Ball (1999), i.e., establishing that the exchange rate variable parameter is negative; this means that a 10% appreciation implies that the central banker must reduce the interest rate 0.53% in the case of the proposal for this research's BANXICO reaction function without the compensation established by Ball (1999) and the inclusion of lagged exchange rate for a period, i.e., the coefficient of

---

[31]If the parameter is zero, we would be in the presence of a monetary rule with the characteristics as proposed by Taylor in 1993 (with the difference that the output gap is not included).

the type of change left behind in a period would offset the reduction of 0.53% of the interest rate.[32]

It continues with the presentation of the remaining specification tests, so Table 5.1 should be checked, which concludes that the estimate is not stable to 95%of confidence, but if it is 90%, it is stable. In addition, it behaves normally since the probability of the Jarque–Bera statistic is 0.60. Also, as mentioned above, the model records autocorrelation, since the probability of statistical Lagrange Multiplier test is zero. Finally, it shows that the estimation of equation (5.14) presents constant variance, that is, homoskedasticity is associated with statistical probability of 0.17.

TABLE 5.1   The Specification Tests for Equation (5.14)

Test	Statistic	Probability
Linearity	Ramsey-RESET	0.03
	4.98	
Normality	Jarque–Bera	0.6073
	0.99	
Autocorrelation	LM test	0.0000
	112.5	
Heteroskedasticity	ARCH	0.1784
	1.64	

Abbreviations: RESET, Regression Equation Specification Error Test; LM, Lagrange Multiplier test; ARCH, autoregressive conditional heteroskedasticity.
Source: Homemade

5.3   EVALUATION

To create the form or the mechanism by which the BANXICO manipulates its instrument of monetary policy, it is necessary to suggest a reaction

---

[32]The reduction of the nominal short-term interest rates is the mechanism to mitigate the contractive effects of an appreciation on aggregate demand. Appreciation makes the external goods cheaper and internally more expensive, resulting in a reduction in net exports. The reduction in the interest rate makes the contraction smaller.

function, which, in a way, is outlined in Section 5.2 of this chapter. The function that is closest to the one used most often in the majority of central banks in the world is the rule raised by Taylor in 1993 and that, along this research, has expanded its description, analysis, controversies, deviations, and virtues.

It is suggested that an equation reacts by changing the short-term nominal interest rate (i_t) when the rate of inflation observed (π_t) is not equal to the inflation targeting (π_t^*). Also, this equation answers when the observed product (y_t) is different from the potential product (y_t^*). This implies that the equation includes in its structure a gap of inflation and another product. The values of the coefficients β and γ mean that weighting is given to each gap and their estimation will be then according to the period of analysis of this document. In addition, the natural balance of long-term interest rate is included in the equation (α)

$$i_t = \alpha + \beta\left(\pi_t - \pi_t^*\right) + \gamma(y_t - y_t^*). \qquad (5.14a)$$

This work, in addition to the components of equation (5.14a) includes, in the Mexican case and common in the literature of monetary policy rules, the lagging nominal interest rate. The number of lags conventionally used is one, to consider the inertial process of that variable. Therefore, the rule estimated in equation (5.15) is *backward looking* and is estimated by ordinary least squares. It should be noted that it is also possible to introduce in the rule future terms for the inflation rate to make the nature of the rule *forward-looking*

$$i_t = \alpha + \beta\left(\pi_t - \pi_t^*\right) + \gamma\left(y_t - y_t^*\right) + i_{t-1} + u_t. \qquad (5.15)$$

The series used in equation (5.13) were consulted from the historical statistics published by the BANXICO and Instituto Nacional de Estadística y Geografía (INEGI) for the period ranging from 2001:01 to 2012:03. The used series have a monthly regularity: the short-term interest rate is the Tasa de Interes Interbancario de Equilibrio or Interbank Equilibrium Interest Rate (TIIE) of 28 days,[33] the inflation rate was obtained from the INPC, for the target of inflation the value of 3% was fixed, while the product was

---

[33]Unlike previous work, the present will include an analysis of the behavior of the BANXICO, using the target rate posted from 2008 by the same issuing institute.

determined by the IGAE, and potential product was obtained using the Hodrick–Prescott filter since it's a nonobservable variable.

Immediately, it was verified if the series are stationary tests for unit roots and it was concluded that the series of rate of interest, inflation gap, and the output gap are actually stationary. The following results are obtained from running the model for four subperiods: 2001:01–2003:03, 2003:04–2005:03, 2005:04–2007:12, and 2008–2012. There is however a general period ranging from 2001:01 to 2008:12, which is represented below:

$$i_t = 2.46 + 0.52\left(\pi_t - \pi_t^*\right) - 0.04\left(y_t - y_t^*\right) + 0.86i_{t-1} + u_t, \quad (5.16)$$

S.D.: (0.66) (0.23) (0.028) (0.029),
Prob.: [**0.0004**] [0.0296] [0.1426] [**0.0000**],
R^2=0.90,
DW=1.89.

Using the form of the break-through of inflation, the inflation rate yields the following results.

$$i_t = 1.06 - 0.016\left(\pi_t - \pi_t^*\right) - 0.047\left(y_t - y_t^*\right) + 0.868i_{t-1} + u_t, \quad (5.16a)$$

S.D.: (0.29) (0.05) (0.028) (0.04),
Prob.: [**0.0005**] [0.75] [0.1029] [**0.0000**],
R^2=0.89,
DW=1.94.

The estimate obtained from the coefficients of equation (5.16) allows to observe the weight that the Mexican issuing institution gives to inflation and product gaps. It is evident that this equation, which seeks a systematic component similar to a monetary policy rule, does not meet by far the Taylor principle, since the coefficient of the inflation gap is less than unity (0.52); however, it is statistically significant with a probability of [0.0296].

The empirical evidence presented enables assertions such as the BANXICO does not use monetary means of stabilization and systematization, as suggested by John Taylor. This is noted by checking the coefficient of the product, which is a negative gap (–0.04). This means that Mexican monetary authorities only have concentrated their efforts on controlling and anchoring of prices, i.e., the inflation gap, subtracting or removing the importance given to the management of the output gap. It is pertinent to state that the model estimated in advance presents a problem to be considered, which is that it does not meet the assumption of permanence of the parameters.

This implies that throughout the analysis period, the Mexican economy registered conjuncture of internal and external events, which caused this problem in the estimation of the model, in particular, the existence of structural changes in the sample. For this reason and to eliminate this problem, equation (5.16) was applied in four subsamples of the original analysis period.

Table 5.2 considered, from the point of view of this study, the changes made by the central bank's monetary policy reaction function. The first subsample starts in 2001:01, when inflation targeting is made official, and ends in 2003:03; it is observed that it starts the trend to the statistical significance of the gap of inflation with a probability of [0.0657] and also shows that the coefficient of the output gap is negative, implying that the central institution does not react to the output gap (however, the coefficient is statistically significant).

The second subsample starts when the monetary authorities altered the regime of accumulating the daily balances, 2003:04–2005:03. The main conclusion of this period is that the central bank reacts to both gaps, although responses to the output gap are hardly significant and even that gap coefficient is not significant, while the other gap coefficient is significant, at 10%, with a probability of [0.0554]. The case of the subsample number three, between 2005:04 and 2007:12, is particularly rare because the central bank reaction function does not react to any of the gaps; however, all of the coefficients are significant, so the results of this subperiod are not conclusive.

Characteristics of the coefficients of the last subsample are that the central bank responded to both gaps; however, the parameter of the inflation gap (0.07) is not significant [0.3269], while the coefficient of the product (0.03) is [0.0000]. This means, in my opinion, that due to the financial crisis that began in 2007 and the economic crisis in 2008, the Mexican Government's efforts are focused on the implementation of countercyclical policies, leaving price controls momentarily without being seen, measures obviously brought about by realizing that it is not out of control due to potential risks that inflation expectations arrive, in the long run, to their permanent target of 3% plus-minus a variation of 1%.

From my point of view, the analyzed period closest to describing a behavior of the Taylor rule is the first (2001:01–2003:03). This is due to the fact that, it is at that moment that BANXICO officially adopts the IT and the eyes of world opinion are on the central banking and the political Constitution of Mexico and the USA. Mexican authorities could not stray too far from what is called a good practice of monetary policy. That is why coefficients of the gap of inflation (at least to 90% of confidence) and product are statistically significant.

TABLE 5.2 Mexico Bank Reaction Function, 2001–2012

Subsample[a]	α	β	γ	i_{t-1}
2001:01–2003:03	5.25	1.47	−0.18	0.83
	−1.996	−0.762	−0.079	−0.06
	[0.0149]	[0.0657]	[0.0337]	[0.0000]
2003:04–2005:03	3.32	0.99	0.00009	0.9
	−1.464	−0.491	−0.065	−0.103
	[0.0344]	[0.0554]	[0.9989]	[0.0000]
2005:04–2007:12	0.23	−0.08	0	0.94
	−0.32	−0.09	−0.011	−0.029
	[0.4831]	[0.3573]	[0.8803]	[0.0000]
2008:01–2012:03[b]	0.31	0.07	0.03	0.97
	−0.223	−0.069	−0.006	−0.017
	[0.1697]	[0.3269]	[0.0000]	[0.0000]

[a]The second and third rows of each period correspond to the standard deviations and the probability of the statistic t, respectively.

[b]This is the period corresponding to the subprime crisis with its epicenter in the USA and represents the central part of this research.

Source: Compilation with data from the Banco de México and Instituto Nacional de Estadística y Geografía (INEGI). With permission

It only remains to check the lagging terms contained in the proposed rule in equation (5.15), i.e., the rate of the previous period. The term coefficients indicate that the BANXICO response is not significant and that it does not react immediately to the policy decisions. It is worth mentioning that when the parameter value is less than unity, then there is a stable path or stable behavior. This is the case of all the revised subsamples. It is recognized by this research that even though during the study period, inflation has been low and stable, it did not follow the "principle of Taylor." This is one of the reasons why I consider that the management of the central bank has been inadequate due to recurrent breaches in achieving the inflation targeting.

Within the framework of policy rules, such as the one proposed in Section 5.3 of this thesis, one can include variables that could affect the short-term interest rate, such as the type of change, the foreign interest rate, etc. The lack of compliance with the principle of Taylor can be associated with the events caused by the recent crises. The most relevant previous estimates and final conclusion is "possible" recognition that the management of the BANXICO does not takes place through the implementation of a Taylor rule.

Now, Table 5.2A records the same estimates as Table 5.2, but with the difference that to form the gap of inflation, the rate of inflation of the following results are obtained. What is relevant here is that the coefficient of the inflation gap (0.05) becomes not significant [0.75], which indicates that the issuing institution of Mexico does not react to the inflation gap. In my opinion, this is a little encouraging result since it is clear that BANXICO devotes all its resources and efforts to the maintenance of the stability of prices, therefore the estimate for all periods analyzed gives results that are not relevant or useful to make some kind of inference.

However, I must conclude that given the above scenario, evaluation for the determination of a systematic component that describes the behavior of BANXICO must agree that it is not possible to establish it. It is not possible, at least by the methodology used for this research. Therefore, we shall announce a possible extension of this research with postsession documents, orders, searches, and extracts, such as the conduct under which our issuing institute is steered. Also included is an additional estimate that used the inflation for the determination of the inflation gap, as shown below.

TABLE 5.2A Mexico Bank Reaction Functions (Using the Inflation), 2001–2012

Subsample[a]	α	β	γ	i_{t-1}
2001:01–2003:03	1.6	0.05	−0.17	0.79
	−0.72	−0.16	−0.08	−0.09
	[0.036]	[0.75]	[0.05]	[0.0000]
2003:04–2005:03	0.74	−0.04	−0.006	0.9
	−0.8	−0.5	−0.07	−0.15
	[0.36]	[0.92]	[0.93]	[0.0000]
2005:04–2007:12	0.4	0.19	0.01	0.92
	−0.2	−0.056	−0.009	−0.024
	[0.05]	[0.0015]	[0.26]	[0.0000]
2008:01–2012:03[b]	0.007	−0.08	0.02	1.0
	−0.1	−0.03	−0.006	−0.02
	[0.94]	[0.03]	[0.0000]	[0.0000]

[a]The second and third rows of each period correspond to the standard deviations and the probability of the statistic t, respectively.

[b]This is the period corresponding to the subprime crisis with its epicenter in the USA and represents the central part of this research.

Source: Compilation with data from the Banco de México and INEGI. With permission

Obviously, the results are far less encouraging than those obtained by the previous estimate. There is evidence of further lack of mentioned parameters and looking out for the systematic component since the coefficient of the output gap is reduced below unity, which allows concluding that definitely BANXICO is not guided by the principle of Taylor. In addition, through this form of estimation, this coefficient becomes not significant statistically, so it is clear that the previous estimate is handicapped significantly.

Motives and previous arguments give cause to what is chosen as the main estimate to the first one. It will now be determined if TIIE series, inflation gap, and the output gap are stationary. To this end, the following hypothesis

contrasts: H_0: $\delta = 0$ and H_1: $\delta = 0$, through the application of two so-called
evidence of unit roots that incorporates in its conceptualization the presence of
autocorrelation. This allows not making mistakes in regards to the existence of
unit roots in the series of the variables used. The tests used for the determination of existence or otherwise of unit roots are the augmented Dickey–Fuller
(ADF)[34] and the Phillips–Perron (PP) tests, applied to equation (5.16). The
results are reported in Table 5.3 and all models of both tests are presented.

TABLE 5.3   Evidence of Unit Roots of Equation (5.16)

Variables	Augmented Dickey–Fuller			Phillips–Perron		
	A	B	C	A	B	C
TIIE	–4.7037	–4.6426	–3.0160	–4.5805	–4.6005	–2.7433
	[0.0001]	[0.0013]	[0.0028]	[0.0002]	[0.0015]	[0.0063]
GAP_Y	–2.4567	–2.4384	–2.4732	–7.2729	–7.2448	–7.3007
	[0.1287]	[0.3582]	[0.0135]	[0.0000]	[0.0000]	[0.0000]
GAP_P	–2.3088	–2.4224	–0.0457	–6.9809	–6.9345	–0.0609
	[0.1708]	[0.3662]	[0.6955]	[0.0000]	[0.0000]	[0.6607]
TIIE (-1)	–4.5907	–4.4225	–3.1070	–4.5286	–4.3956	–2.8136
	[0.0002]	[0.0028]	[0.0021]	[0.0003]	[0.0031]	[0.0051]

Values in bold denote rejection of the null hypothesis.

The GAP_Y series comprises the differential between the IGAE and potential product
derived from the same series using the Hodrick–Prescott filter, while the GAP_P series is
made up of the inflation from the INPC-target gap fixed inflation of 3%.

0.05% of the test significance; model A includes intercept with a value of –2.8895; the
B model includes trend and intercept with a value in the –3.4535; the C model does not
include either trend or intercept and has the value of –1.94; values in bold denote the
rejection of the null hypothesis.

The values in brackets are the odds of the statistic t.

Source: Homemade

---

[34]This test adds the appropriate number of lags to eliminate autocorrelation.

The stationary nature of the series cannot be validated using the ADF test results, so it was necessary to apply the PP test, which leads to the conclusion that, indeed, the series used TIIE, output gap, inflation, and lagging TIIE gap period, which are stationary.

Finally, Table 5.4 presents an evaluation of two additional subperiods; these subsamples include the temporality of the subprime crisis first and the second covers the aftermath of the crisis, years that are characterized by a period of considerable recession. Reported results again do not identify a systematic behavior; however, this time this result was to be expected already than most of the economies of the world, mainly because the developed and emerging economies implemented contingency plans characterized by essentially countercyclical policies.

TABLE 5.4   Mexico Bank Reaction Functions, 2001–2012

Subsample	α	β	γ	i_{t-1}
2008:01–2010:06	**−0.05**	**−0.1**	**0.03**	**1.02**
	0.16	0.05	0.008	0.02
	0.73	0.06	0.0005	0
2009:10–2012:03	**0.33**	**0.01**	**0.0002**	**0.92**
	0.32	0.008	0.001	0.06
	0.31	0.09	0.8	0.000

[a]The second and third rows of each period correspond to the standard deviations and the probability of the statistic t, respectively.

Source: Compilation with data from the Banco de México and INEGI. With permission

KEYWORDS

- Output gap,
- BANXICO,
- Gap of inflation,
- Balance of risks,
- Taylor rule,
- TIIE

CHAPTER 6

DELINKING OF THE VARIABLE EXCHANGE RATE AS A NOMINAL ANCHOR OF THE ECONOMY IN THE CONDUCT OF MONETARY POLICY IN MEXICO

CONTENTS

The low inflation and the monetary policy that has delivered it have led to lower pass-through through a reduction in the expected persistence of cost and price changes.

—John B. Taylor, 2000

The aim of this section is to provide evidence that in recent years (decade of the 2000s and to date), the transfer of the exchange rate effect is no longer relevant in the process of price formation. The first evidence is that in emerging economies, the behavior of the inflationary variable has changed its course from that of high variability to one of relative stability. This phenomenon coincides with the implementation of the inflation-targeting approach (IT) and the abandonment of the exchange rate as nominal anchor.

For these purposes, literature that indicates the theoretical support for the effects of exchange rate variations – depreciation – on the general level of prices – inflation rate – will be reviewed, passing through several empirical attempts trying to demonstrate the current irrelevance of the effects of the volatility of the exchange rate on the pricing structure. All these culminate with the revision of the estimate of a rule extended from Taylor that includes, as opposed to the rule of Chapter 5, the breakthrough product, inflation, and exchange rate. Hence it derives elements that validate the current disassociation of the behavior of the exchange rate and general inflation in Mexico, as well as a possible adjustment in monetary policy management, i.e., not-so-statistical significance of the gap of the type of change and positivity, as well as significance of the output gap, respectively.

According to Romero (2013), the effect of an exchange rate depreciation on the inflation rate must meet certain assumptions: *i*) existence of total openness to trade in goods and services in the economy; *ii*) all the goods in the economy should be tradable; *iii*) there should be important differences in the homogeneity or substitutability between domestic and imported products; and *iv*) the general index of prices in different countries include the same goods, and these have the same weight. These four conditions form the theory of Purchasing Power Parity (PPP, its acronym in English).

However, the reality is that they are not met because there is presence of nontradable items in the world, differences in the constitution of baskets of goods of the indexes of prices in the countries, as well as heterogeneity of goods, taxes, and marketing costs. The significance of this lies in the interpretation that a variation (overvaluation/devaluation or appreciation/ depreciation, as appropriate) of 1% in the nominal exchange rate implies an increase in the price index to the consumer of ~1%.

"There is evidence for Mexico that in the short-term, the PPP is not met, but that in the long run is doing so" (Romero, 2013). To be more precise, one can only validate the operability of a price in the very long term and in situations of hyperinflation. Following the explanation of Romero (2013), there are two reasons to warn about the lack of effects of variations in the type of change in prices due to the breach of the law in a just price in the short term; these are: *i*) imperfections of microlevel market and *ii*) the presence of tradable and nontradable goods and imported services, as well as relative difference between tradable and nontradable prices at the macrolevel.

It is clear that changes in the exchange rate directly affect the relative price of the imported goods; these disturbances do not necessarily imply that it moved completely to the general level of prices. The above phenomenon has relations with the following: *i*) the central bank's monetary policy strategy. This means that the issuing institution enjoys high credibility and good reputation, and that expectations of economic agents will not be modified by the impact of exchange rate variability; *ii*) according to Taylor (2000), before an exchange rate adjustment, economic agents intending to lower the inflation environment do not have sufficient incentives to modify – climbing – prices.[1]

Also it is necessary to consider *iii*) the behavior of the real exchange rate as an important determinant for the definition of the transfer coefficient (seen in Romero, 2013); *iv*) regardless of the transience or permanence of the volatility of the exchange rate variable, importers must identify the situation before modifying their pricing structure; *v*) the level of economic activity, because it is more difficult to transfer the increase in costs to the bottom end – consumer price – when there is an economic downturn, for instance; *vi*) the degree of market concentration is also involved in the transfer of the exchange rate to prices, since it creates rigidities; and *vii*) if the economy in question has, in addition to the containment of inflation, a wage control policy, then the effect as well as its coefficient will be less.

---

[1]Point (*ii*) is true if and only if economic entities assume the exchange rate adjustment as transitional. For this purpose, it is necessary, as mentioned, that the central bank's monetary policy decisions are backed by high reputation and an acceptable credibility level, which means the monetary policy instrument serves effectively as a nominal anchor of the economy.

Thus, in Table 6.1, data collected from the work of Romero (2013), which deserve to be taken up for further analysis, are presented. It is clear that from 1993 to 2000, he recorded that the maximum monthly exchange rate variation reached levels of 33.83% and maximum monthly inflation was 7.67% for the period 2000–2012; the maximum monthly variation of the exchange rate was just 17.12% and was associated with a maximum monthly inflation of 1.13%. This shows that not only is the price level low and stable but also that the effect of transfer of exchange rate volatility to prices has decreased.

TABLE 6.1   Exchange Rate and Inflation, Mexico, 1993–2000 and 2000–2012 (%)

Period	Variation in the Rate of Exchange (Monthly Maximum)	Variation in the Exchange Rate (Monthly Average)	Inflation (Monthly Maximum)	Inflation (Monthly Average)
1993–2000	33.83	1.46	7.67	1.41
2000–2012	17.12	0.21	1.13	0.37

Source: Compilation based on Romero, J. Es posible utilizar el tipo de cambio para hacer más competitiva la economía mexicana? *El Colegio de México*, Centro de Estudios Económicos, núm. X-2013, 2013.. With permission

Figure 6.1 shows that after the crisis occurred during the second half of 2008, the trend of the exchange rate has been rising; however, the volatility of the exchange rate expressed by its cycle shows a process of containment through interventions in the exchange by the central institution, which, in turn, is consistent with the strategy of monetary policy, i.e., with a focus on inflation targeting, the flexibility of the exchange rate, and a policy rule.

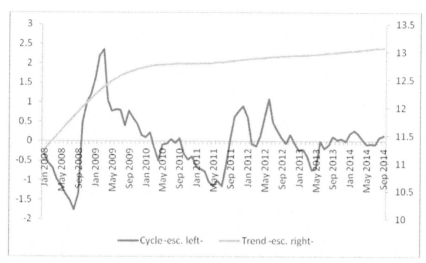

FIGURE 6.1   Trend and the Exchange Rate Cycle, Mexico, 2008–2014.

The Hodrick–Prescott filter is a smoothing method that is widely used among macroeconomists to obtain a smooth estimate of the long-term trend component of a series (lambda = 14,400). esc. = Scale.

(Own elaboration.)

In addition, shown in the same graph is the observation that 2011 and 2012 registered large depreciations of the exchange rate, which also impacted on the behavior of inflation. The above graph is, once again, evidence of the thesis proposed by Taylor (2000), the one that argues that the transfer is low in the presence of an inflationary environment that is low and stable.

The interventions by central banks are not limited to the administration of interest rates as monetary policy instruments. On the contrary, through their central organs and fiscal institutions, governments resort to use of international reserves that, as mentioned above, are mainly accumulated by developing and emerging countries. The above is valid, as reviewed in Chapter 4, for this type of countries, including Mexico, although they claim to international institutions such as the International Monetary Fund that their exchange rate regime is flexible, persisting with what Calvo and Reinhart (2002) called as "fear of floating."

The immediate implication of the above and for the purposes of this research is that the behavior of the exchange rate variable is an issue that the countries concerned have not been able to dissociate from the management of their currency to the exchange rate policy, according to the evidence of Calvo and Reinhart (2002); still, it is a determinant in the decision-making process of the issuing national institutions. If these countries effectively implemented a flexible exchange rate regime, the variability of international reserves should be reduced to zero because there would be no need for the central banks to increase or restrict the availability of dollars in their markets.

This phenomenon has persisted until 2011, as Table 4.1 in Chapter 4 "Fear of Floating in Mexico, 1989–2011" shows; the probability of variation in international reserves, the type of change, and the interest rate were high and rising with floating exchange rate, it means that authorities have little credibility, because the manipulation of interest rates to stabilize the exchange rate variable is very frequent. This mechanism is irrelevant if expectations of inflation – target rate of inflation – and the variations in the exchange rate are not well anchored.

In this case, the presence of a doubling of the nominal anchor of an economy is not compatible with the elements that characterize the IT. This, far from stabilizing the mentioned variables (exchange rate and interest rate), cause monetary authorities to lose credibility, so that the application of "good monetary policy," which is constituted by the use of a monetary policy rule, the formalization of the floating exchange rate, and the implementation of the IT, is not complied with fully.

The previous argument, in the Mexican case, is denied most recently by the research of Cortés in a 2013 paper.[2] In it, are confirmed, in some way, the results of this investigation that the variable exchange rate in Mexico is not decisive as the nominal anchor of the economy; it means that Banco de México (BANXICO) does not provide an exchange rate gap based on its reaction to the effect of the transfer of the rate of exchange on the general price level, which is low. This is sample, as stipulated by Calvo and Reinhart (2002), that in Mexico there is no presence of "fear of floating" because the exchange rate to prices has relatively low transfer coefficient,[3] and the central bank applies the IT and enjoys some credibility.

---

[2]Other works also support the results of cuts (2013), e.g., Capistrán Ibarra, and Ramos France (2012), Chiquiar, Noriega, and Ramos-France (2010), and Santaella (2002), among others.

[3]It is the effect of variations of the rate of exchange on domestic inflation. If approaching unity, it means that the transfer of devaluation or depreciation of the prices is total; furthermore, a near-zero coefficient implies that the elasticity of domestic prices before a change in the nominal exchange rate is null.

According to Cortés (2013), the transfer of the rate of exchange on the general price level is low and statistically nonsignificant, which is validated by the results of the estimation of a Taylor rule for the period 2008–M01 to 2012–M03, which is concluded in a similar way; it means that the exchange rate gap is not only statistically nonsignificant but that its coefficient is not expected according to the Calvo–Reinhart hypothesis. This last is justified in that during the first 10 years of the twenty-first century and the depreciation in 2011,[4] the trajectory of the transfer of the rate of exchange on prices decreased (Cortes, 2013).

Results from Cortes (2013) and the reported review of the first minutes issued by the Mexican central bank until its thirteenth version made by this research are consistent with the observation that "transfer coefficient of disturbance of the exchange rate on the general level of prices to the consumer in Mexico is low and statistically nonsignificant during the period from June 2001 to August 2012" (Cortes 2013) and evidence that exchange rate volatility is reduced considerably – from 0.43 to 0.06 – in the periods ranging from January 2000 to December 2003 and January 2004 to the last month of 2007.

However, this downward trend was not maintained due to the implications of the financial crisis that emerged in the USA; so the volatility of the exchange rate variable increased to 1.29. However, what we want to show here is that, despite high variability of exchange rate, there is no evidence that the transfer of the disturbance of the exchange rate variable is a determinant in the formation of prices in the economy in Mexico. It means that if the exchange rate variability does not affect the National Index of Consumer Prices (Indice Nacional de Precios al Consumidor; INPC), then there is an exchange rate gap,[5] which is used to determine the behavior of the instrument of monetary policy of the central bank, i.e., the interest rate.

The adoption of the IT has resulted in the process by which prices are formed in the Mexican economy and is significantly different from

---

[4]Consequent upon the deterioration of the global economic environment in the second half of 2011, the rate of change in Mexico depreciated considerably. According to BANXICO (2012), the exchange rate had registered more depreciated levels, which was anticipated. "In particular, in mid-2011, the Mexican economy was affected by a crash at the exchange rate as a reflection of the deterioration in the external economic environment, which resulted in a depreciation that came to exceed 18 per cent between July and December of that year" (Cortes, 2013).

[5]The exchange rate gap is the difference between the exchange rate used to settle the liabilities with a monthly target published by the Instituto Nacional de Estadística y Geografía and the representative rate that approximates the trend of the exchange rate calculated by the method of the Hodrick–Prescott filter.

the proposal that "inflation can be characterized as a stationary process" (Chiquiar, Noriega, and Ramos-France, 2010; cited in BANXICO, 2012). The above has to do with the fact that, recently, the review of prices of schemes are carried out by the companies in preset periods, i.e., "time-dependently." This is an indication that agents' economic activity– business – is guided by the announcements and actions of the central bank in terms of its forecasts at both microeconomic and macroeconomic levels.[6]

A further situation that supports the above argument is that, according to BANXICO (2012), during the period 1976–2000, the nominal exchange rate and the INPC were closely correlated – 0.79 coefficient (see Figure 6.2). However, if we review the chart in more detail, it is clear that such correlation lost force since 1994, the year in which the central bank became independent, the transition was made to the flexible exchange rate regime, and the IT was implemented.[7] Having said the above, it is necessary to note that the Mexican Central Bank emphasizes that the correlation was lost in 2000, just before the official adoption of the IT.

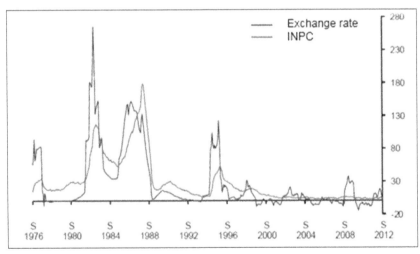

FIGURE 6.2 National Index of Consumer Prices (Indice Nacional de Precios al Consumidor) and Exchange Rate, Mexico, 1976–2012.

(From BANXICO, 2012. With permission.)

---

[6]This also implies that every time they have left to take action at its discretion, it means. already reviews of prices depending on the circumstances they face are not made the company – state-dependent way

[7]Through the use of monetary policy instruments – the nominal variable – as net credit, accrued balances, and the nominal interest rate.

The above statement is confirmed by the argument of that same BANXICO that from 2001, the degree of correlation between the processes of depreciation and inflation decreased (0.36) and validates the proposition that the effect of transfer of variations in the exchange rate to prices is low. "In particular, you can see that 2008–2009 depreciation did not have important effects on inflation, in contrast to the devaluations in 1976–1977, 1982–1983, 1987–1988, and 1995, which were followed by significant increases in inflation" (BANXICO, 2012).

Thus, following the argument of BANXICO, the research reviewed the most recent rate of annual variations of the INPC and the annual exchange rate, behaviors, and relationships shown in Figure 6.3.[8] The change in the relationship shown in Figure 6.2 is derived from the inflation of Bank of Mexico's report for July–September of 2012, which, in turn, was extracted from Cortes (2013).

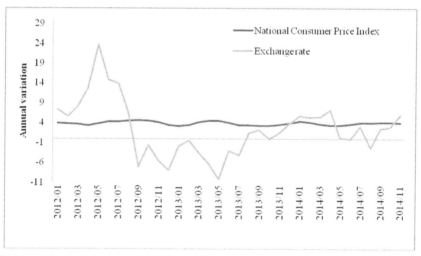

FIGURE 6.3 National Index of Consumer Prices (Indice Nacional de Precios al Consumidor) and Exchange Rate, Mexico, 2012–2014.

Monthly National Consumer Price Index. General index and objective expenditure (second half of December 2010 = 100 base points) and type of weight change with respect to the dollar (banking, wholesale).

(Own elaboration with Instituto Nacional de Estadística y Geografía (INEGI) data. With permission.)

---

[8]This graph is an update of that provided in BANXICO (2012) and Cortes (2013). Even with the expansion of the sample until November 2014, the interpretation persists.

The above is evidence that the depreciation recorded in 2012[9] was not accompanied by significant increases in overall inflation. It also suggests that in an environment of stability of prices at low levels, the transfer of variations in the exchange rate to prices in Mexico is low. "In particular, the depreciation that occurred between 2008 and 2009 does not seem to have had important effects on inflation, in contrast to the above-mentioned devaluations" (Cortés, 2013).

Even if we review the same graph, posed in a different way, one can see that not only is the correlation minimal, the behaviors of annual variations of both INPC and the exchange rate are the opposite (see Figure 6.4). Then, we cannot say that the exchange rate is stable; on the other hand, it has turned out to be very volatile, in the first month of 2012 through 2014, mainly in mid-2012 and eleventh month, and from mid-2014 to date; however, once again the volatility of the INPC was "small."

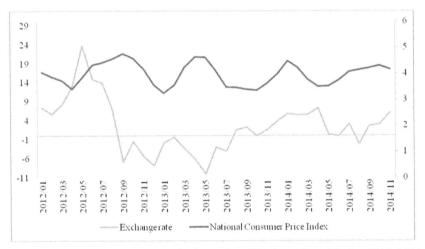

FIGURE 6.4   Annual Variations (%) in the INPC and Exchange Rate, Mexico, 2012–2014.

Monthly National Consumer Price Index. General index and expenditure (second half of December 2010 = 100 base points) and type of weight change with respect to the dollar (banking, wholesale).

(Own elaboration with Instituto Nacional de Estadística y Geografía (INEGI) data. With permission.)

---

[9]On June 8, 2012 was held the twelfth minutes of decision of monetary policy in Mexico, which is subtracted, in terms of the risks to the rise in inflation, which the Board pointed out that it has been observed a slight transfer effect of the inflation rate. However, he warned that if this situation (the depreciated peso) pressures and the effects of change on inflation will begin to be considered dangerous or harmful.

The Mexican-type small and open economies are highly sensitive to volatilities in the behavior of macroeconomic variables such as the exchange rate, the stance of monetary policy of the central bank, public spending strategy, and ads regarding the economic performance – growth, employment, among others – from countries such as the USA, Germany, and, recently, China. Obviously, because in the global economy, the source of power is still the fossil (hydrocarbons), the structure of prices of this *commodity* is a variable that the governments of countries monitor, mainly those who in addition to consumers are producers, as in the case of Mexico. This is why we provide a brief account of the implications of changes in the international price of oil.

Recently, in the Mexican case, not only has the market value of petroleum been revised downward but a planned fall in production has also been registered, given the high dependency of the country on oil revenues, with likely fiscal problems even with oil hedges contracted by the Government, since they will only be able to cover a third of the estimated production made. This connection ensures that an import of refined products is considerably cheaper. The above produces effects in both directions, *i*) as mentioned, likely cuts to public spending in 2015 or 2016 and *ii*) imports of gasoline savings, mainly.

However, this decline in prices will have an impact on the implementation of the recently approved energy reform because one of its components emphasizes the generation of incentives so that national or foreign investors decide to explore and produce in active oil tankers that are part of the country's proven and probable reserves. Note that this category aims to reverse the considerable fall in production, taking advantage of the low costs of production, since the bulk of national production recorded a cost of between $9 and $15 per barrel (El Economista, 2015).

Another relevant connection is one in which the cheapest prices of inputs (oil) directly affect economic activity and also benefiting countries like Mexico and, in the short term, the performance of Mexican exports will be improved. However, the concern regarding cuts in public spending persists, which, according to the Financial Times (2014), for every dollar that drops in the price of a barrel of oil, collection of the Secretaría de Hacienda y Crédito Público decreases by approximately $300 million.

As seen in the review, there are both negative and positive aspects about the fall of international oil price; however, if this trend persists and due to the high dependence on revenues derived from oil of Mexico, the country is in many ways more vulnerable and there is the possibility of the Government contracting debt while the current debt is already high and more attractive in relation to recent years.

Once posed in general terms, the effect of economies such as the Mexican on the variable of the price of hydrocarbons takes up the central theme of this section. As has been explained, "the transfer coefficient perturbations of the exchange rate on the general level of prices to the consumer in Mexico is low and statistically nonsignificant during the period from June 2001 to August 2012." However, it should be mentioned that this transfer is positive and significant for the prices of the goods (Cortés, 2013).[10] This author reaches these conclusions through the estimation of a model of vector autoregression.

One of the qualities of this type of models is that it is possible to analyze the dynamics among a set of variables considered endogenous.[11] Note that in part of the course of the article, it means, that it included as endogenous variables – Mexico –[12] and exogenous variables – USA,[13] only the latter can affect domestic activity because it's a model that considers Mexico as an accepting price economy. To be more specific, the main findings of Cortes (2013) are, despite the exchange rate depreciation of 2011, although cumulative transfer elasticity increased slightly in the last month of 2010 to the eighth month of 2012, the effect remains statistically nil.

Thus, to make the point even clearer, the delinking of the exchange rate variable in the process of formation of prices in the Mexican economy and, therefore, as the nominal anchor of the economy in the conduct of monetary policy in Mexico, we relied on the results of Capistrán et al. (2012), which, basically, indicate that the elasticity of transfer of the variations of the rate of exchange on the general INPC, for the period 2001–2010, was 0.02 and 0.05 in the short (12 months) and long terms (48 months), respectively, and both impacts were found to be statistically significant.

However, findings from Cortes (2003) suggest that for the extension of the period until August 2012, elasticity of transfer was the same in the short term, i.e., 0.02 and, in the long term, it was 0.07; however, this increase was not significant. Only in the case of nonfood goods, the transfer

---

[10]The significance of the transfer of goods prices was caused specifically by the nonfood goods, since the price of these is mainly determined in the international market.

[11]Works from 2001 because, according to Chiquiar et al. (2010), starting from that year, it went to behave as a stochastic process with stationary trend.

[12]IGAE, Certificados de la Tesoreria de la Federación (CETES) 28, exchange rate, and INPC.

[13]Industrial production of US rate of treasuries per month, consumer price index, index of European Union, and international prices of the raw materials index.

coefficient of the variable exchange rate to prices is statistically different from zero in the long run, i.e., significant.

There has been evidence that the exchange rate has been losing its influence on prices. Therefore, one can argue that while there are interventions by the central bank on the foreign exchange market, this variable is not decisive for the decision making of monetary policy in the country. Therefore, conditions for implementing the "good monetary policy" in Mexico are suitable, i.e., one with a flexible managed – but increasingly less relevant type, the continuous search for price stability through IT, credibility of monetary policy, and, particularly, by anchoring inflation expectations through of target rate of inflation.

It only remains to identify the systematic component that BANXICO uses, it means, the specificity of the monetary rule by which it is managed. However, it will be necessary for other works, so we will present another type of evidence that will reinforce the argument that the effect transfer of exchange rate already it is not relevant in determining the monetary policy of Mexico, however, it monitors the latter. Because it is a safe topic, in the minutes of the Bank of Mexico, they indicated that this variable corresponds to another type of risk[14] that it could affect inflation in addition to agricultural prices and raw materials, for example. However, they make special emphasis at all times in the evolution of inflation expectations.

This type of evidence shows that, apart from the transfer coefficient of the rate of exchange on the general price level, nothing significant has been done despite various processes of depreciation of the national currency; thus, something similar will happen when trying to include in the estimate of Taylor's rule for Mexico that includes an exchange rate gap. It proposes to add this component to the original equation by Taylor (1993), in addition to its product and inflation gaps, because they suggest as discussed in the minutes of the Mexican central institution.[15]

In addition, as already reviewed in Chapter 5 of this work, the estimation of equation (5.3c) was done from statistically significant coefficients of the gap of inflation and the exchange rate gap. It should be noted that the former is higher than unity, which means that you are approaching the

---

[14]The members of the Board of Governors indicated that the behavior of the exchange rate is a determinant of the reduction of inflation (Banco de Mexico, 2011d) and that a limited volatility of the exchange rate variable contributes to the reduction in tradable price inflation. Note that then, some Board members recognized that stable exchange rate has been a favorable factor in the performance of inflation but that it could be reversed in the future, as it is happening now (Banco de Mexico, 2011f).
[15]In the minutes of July 20, 2012, the Board unanimously noted the existence of a trend toward the depreciation of the peso against the dollar.

rule established by Taylor in the beginning, and the second, that it turned out to be negative. As you can see, this equation does not consider the output gap since it wanted to detect a systematic component according to that established in the minutes of the Bank of Mexico. As mentioned, this model presented autocorrelation so, to get to another type of evidence or relevant findings, we should adjust it and include the break-through product.

Then arises equation (6.1), which is general and specifies, for the purposes of model fit, that it was without constant

$$i_t = \alpha + \beta_1\left(E_t\left[\pi_t - \pi_t^*\right]\right) + \beta_2\left(E_t\left[y_t - y_t^*\right]\right) + \beta_3\left(E_t\left[e_o - e^R\right]\right) + i_{t-1} + D_{\text{structural}} + u_t, \quad (6.1)$$

where

α: is the equilibrium real interest rate over the long term;

β_1: measures the response of the central bank to deviations of inflation on your target;

β_2: measures the reaction of monetary authorities to deviations of the product with respect to the potential product; and

β_3: measures the sensitivity of the issuing institution to deviations of exchange rate observed with respect to the representative exchange rate.

The period of analysis for the estimation of this rule of policy currency is the type of Taylor (1993) but increased as it goes from 2008:01 to 2012:03 and used the following series. For π_t, the annualized inflation rate, for y_t, the index of global economic activity (Indicador Global de la Actividad Económica, IGAE), for e_o, the type of change in pesos per dollar to settle liabilities denominated in foreign currency, and to i_{t-1}, the lagging nominal interest rate. Both potential output y_t^* and the representative exchange rate e^R were derived using the Hodrick–Prescott filter.[16] The specification of this rule of monetary policy for the Mexican case in the first month of 2008 to the third month of 2012 includes a dichotomous variable that captures the shock caused by the structural change of the depreciation of 2008 M01–2009 M05, explained previously.

Below are the results of this estimation:

$$i_t = 0.092\left(E_t\left[\pi_t - \pi_t^*\right]\right) + 0.038\left(E_t\left[y_t - y_t^*\right]\right) + 0.044\left(E_t\left[e_o - e^R\right]\right) + 1.04i_{t-1} + D_{\text{structural}} + u_t. \quad (6.2)$$

---

[16]The operator's expectations, E_t, is used in the reaction function simply to specify that it is a function that looks forward (*forward looking*).

As you can see, the coefficient of the inflation gap is positive and statistically significant at 10% – 0.091; however, it does not coincide with the theoretically expected value; it has to be greater than unity – near 1.5 – to make it consistent with Taylor's principle. In addition, the coefficient of the product also proved to be surprisingly and significantly positive – 0.000. However, according to Ramos-France and Torres (2005), if coefficients of inflation and product gaps are positive, then the rule is consistent with the IT,[17] so the inclusion of the exchange rate gap is redundant since the instrument of monetary policy, through a target for the inflation rate, effectively serves as the nominal anchor of the economy.

The revised paragraph, in turn, implies that while maintaining continuous monitoring of the exchange rate variable, this variable performance is disconnected from the conduct of the monetary policy of the Mexican issuing institution. Unlike the model estimated in Chapter 5, this includes the gap of the exchange rate, which is not statistically significant – 0.149 – due to the loss of weight of the effect of transfer of the variability of the exchange rate on the formation of prices, which was explained along this section. Finally, both the backlog of lagging nominal interest rate and the *dummy* variable are statistically significant – 0.000 and 0.028, respectively – so it helped to fit the model.[18]

To conclude, the evidence shown indicates that in Mexico, the transfer effect turns out to be low since the adoption of IT, which was corroborated with the lack of statistical significance of the coefficient of the perturbations of the exchange rate on the general formation of prices. Also, the Mexican experience confirms the loss of importance of the exchange rate variable on the management of BANXICO, which means that the fall of the exchange transfer coefficient to the inflation rate is consistent with the extrication of the exchange rate variable as a nominal anchor of the economy in the conduct of monetary policy in Mexico.

---

[17]The relevance that the output gap is positive and statistically significant is that it is possible that the BANXICO reaction function has modifications, at least temporarily, because of the situation of the crisis of 2008–2009. This occurs despite the fact that the main objective of the Mexico Bank is to maintain the purchasing power of the currency and price stability. It will certainly be interesting to assess the effects of this situation and test whether the issuing Mexican institution cares about the performance of the product at the hour of their decision making through positivity and significance of the output gap. The statistical significance of the product can be explained by the use of countercyclical policies to mitigate the effects of the crisis at the end of the past decade. Because of this, this will be the focus of an investigation in the future.

[18]In terms of testing residual behavior, it behaves normally to the 5% level – with a probability of 0.125 – and presents no autocorrelation at 10% – 0.010. It has however, heteroskedasticity, implying that the estimators lose efficiency but are consistent and unbiased.

The findings do not suggest that the fall observed in the transfer coefficient can be considered permanent. If the level of the inflation rate and its persistence are elevated in the future, it is likely that new increases are recorded in the transfer coefficient, which, in turn, would put into question the efforts of the central banker due to the fact that if the exchange rate again becomes influential in the determination of short-term interest rate, one would be in the presence of a double-nominal anchor of the economy.

KEYWORDS

- **Exchange rate,**
- **Purchasing Power Parity**
- **INPC, Hodrick–Prescott filter**
- **Oil revenues, price index**

CONCLUSIONS

The development of this research paper is based broadly on the acceptance of the hypothesis of rational expectations (HER). This is so, since it is recognized that the basic work of the central banks of the world is precisely a part of the so-called incorporation process or the methodology of modeling to this hypothesis. In this process, theoretical aspects that have proved to be fundamental to the modern monetary theory have emanated. I specifically refer to concepts like the natural rate of unemployment, which in my opinion laid the groundwork for the elaboration of a work such as that of Kydland and Prescott's dynamic inconsistency, where stands the supremacy of cooperative solutions.

Likewise, the HER has been crucial for other works, such as that by Barro and Gordon (1983), with its inflationary surprises and benefit analysis, manner of operating, and its effects in different types of countries. However, this assumption has been the subject of many objections that demonstrate the weaknesses and insufficiencies of those authors such as Amartya Sen (1977), Modigliani (1985), and Tobin (1980). Even with the theoretical difficulties that rational expectations faced, it can still serve as a pillar of what today is known as "good monetary policy." The above is determined by three essential components, two of which are part of this work.

A better monetary practice is implemented by a Trinity of elements, in what is known as the Taylor *tripod*. It is structured by a regime of floating exchange rate, an aspect that, from my perspective, serves as a prerequisite for the second step of the *tripod*, which is the inflation-targeting approach, which is used as a nominal anchor for the economy to the nominal interest rate. This is why the exchange rate regime should be flexible and not duplicate efforts for the anchoring of the economy and, most importantly, should not insert uncertainty with respect to the actions of the central bank but should strengthen the credibility and reputation of the same.

The remaining aspect is concerned with the rules of monetary policy that limit the discretion of the monetary authorities to short-term events. The use of rules for monetary policy has spread across the length and breadth of the planet thanks to the contribution of John Taylor, who proposed a rule that bears his name. Its use, or some variation of it, has spread in the majority of central banks around the world in a timely manner depending on the requirements of each country. However, it is pertinent to point out that the basis of that rule is to regulate the decision in terms of monetary policy between a gap of inflation reduction and a break-through product.

Another feature of the rule is that it gives the same weight to each gap. The above could be subject to misinterpretation, such as assuming that the central bank operates with a dual mandate. Given the above and to clarify the point of the institutional mandate, an additional concept to the rule emerges; I am referring to the principle of Taylor as evidence by using a function of reaction that the central banks that have opted to use this policy mechanism actually operate using a hierarchical command. This means that the coefficient of the inflation gap is larger than unity (1.5), while that of the output gap is less than one (0.5).

One of the variations of the rule of Taylor that was worth reviewing and that is reflected in Minutes and Reaction Function of Chapter 5 is the inclusion of the exchange rate variable to the same rule structure. This change is particularly efficient in developing and emerging countries due to the fact that these countries still have a high effect transfer of the exchange rate to prices, which is justified by the hypothesis raised by Calvo and Reinhart of fear to float. However, the huge popularity of this mechanism (policy rules) in limiting the discretionary actions of monetary authorities presents a set valid objection, listed below, as designated. Most relevant criticisms made to the use of monetary policy rules are detailed in Developments and Controversies of Chapter 3 of this document; however, we must emphasize some of them since they were situations that I came across during the conduct of this research work.

The main one, was in my opinion, the difficulty of measuring potential output, since this is an unobservable variable, and it was questioned why forecasts for inflation are not incorporated to provide the same flexibility rule, etc. But the limitations of the rule of monetary proposed by John Taylor, also presents virtues to consider. The most important, from my perspective, is that it serves the role of reference and provides an analytical framework for the decision-making authorities; another role is to increase the transparency and credibility of the central bank and, therefore, improve its reputation.

The revision of the Taylor rule that was made in this work was to de-termine the existence or absence of a systematic component in the work-ing of the BANXICO or if it is indeed guided by the Taylor rule. During the period analyzed, there are two phases: *i*) the first of these is when the policy instrument comprised accumulated balances; and *ii*) in the second phase, daily accumulated balances were used. This then determined that the Banco de México reacted in different ways to the gaps and identified that as of 2001, in the third month of 2003, the Mexican issuing institu-tion was guided by what seems to be the beginning of the Taylor rule, at least in regard to the inflation gap; however, the product gap coefficient is negative.

This suggests that the BANXICO, during the official adoption of the inflation-targeting approach, effectively tried to adhere to norms as dic-tated by the Taylor rule, but this caused the nature of its mandate to be very clear. This is mentioned because the negativity of the coefficient of the valid output gap in relation to the mandate that our central bank is guided is unique, which is consistent with the provisions of our Consti-tution. Well, the analyzed evidence for the following periods establishes that any systematic behavior was not detected or recorded since the co-efficients of both gaps are not significant or are not consistent with the theoretically expected value; so, it is seen that the rule of Taylor has not been followed strictly. It is clear that the efforts of the BANXICO have focused exclusively on inflation control; however, the assessment in this document of the inflation targeting used in the analysis period yields re-sults that validate those obtained in the evaluation of the rules. I mean essentially that there is credibility, pursuant to the test of Svensson, in the initial period, one in which performance was recorded by the policy rule, limiting the discretionary actions. Therefore, my sample thesis finds that the BANXICO applied most of the time the so-called good monetary policy; this means that following the principle of Taylor (in some way) ensured that its inflation targeting was credible to economic agents.

Also this thesis argues that only in the period or subsample ranging from 2001 to 2003 did it attack the problem of dynamic inconsistency in a focused, efficient, and effective manner, except that this was the period in which Taylor approaches were implemented for the first time jointly. What this means is that it is very likely that this result has been obtained since the issuing institution wished to note that the precepts of "good monetary policy" were carried out.

This policy was led by a flexible-type foreign exchange regime and the presence of a political ruler, which are framed the under inflation-targeting approach. Inflation targeting is also subject to several observations relating to its functioning and operation. Criticism that attacks inflation targeting with greater severity is that is too much rigid, only considering inflation and allocating all the efforts of the central bank for the achievement of the objectives relating to prices, at the expense of real variables such as product or use.

However, proponents of the approach argue that the lack of flexibility that is mentioned is serviced through responses to short-term shocks, allowing a move away from the target of inflation. Nevertheless, the situation in which the observed inflation moves away from the target is to be announced and justified. A second objection to inflation targeting is that its performance, that is, both the monetary rules of the approach design, was aimed at solving the problems of developed countries.

Note that throughout this research, we not only assessed both ends of the *tripod* of Taylor, policy rules, and inflation targeting, but we also carried out a test of the hypothesis of fear to float of Calvo and Reinhart. Thus, we highlight the effects of having a fixed price of the currency to imply import credibility from the country whose currency is used as reference. However, the fixed parity is weakened when faced with speculative attacks, banking and financial crises, during the opening and liberalization process, which involves, among other things, increased mobility of capital. These are some reasons why the majority of the world's countries opted for a flexible exchange rate regime. Also, setting the parity is incompatible with inflation targeting because it would be doubling the nominal anchors of the economy.

Now, the proposition of flexible exchange rates removed rigidities in the implementation of monetary policy, thus discarding the possibility of subordination to another country and granting capabilities to the monetary authorities to deal with external shocks. Given the above, the Calvo–Reinhart hypothesis states that some countries, especially the emerging ones, dislike a high inflation rate. This means that the possible interventions carried out in the foreign exchange market and other variables are primarily due to fear of inflation. However, the Calvo–Reinhart hypothesis allows to present evidence that, indeed, Mexico is an example of developing countries that have been susceptible to fear to float. This is because the credibility and reputation of its monetary institutions are not sufficient to eliminate, once the transfer of the exchange rate to prices is effected.

This thesis, since its beginning, argued that too much emphasis on the tip of the exchange rate of the *tripod* of Taylor would not be productive. The above is derived from the premise that, in my opinion, the exchange rate should be flexible before one thinks of any policy rule and, of course, of target given to inflation. Therefore, the implementation of rules and inflation targeting happens once the exchange rate regime is of the floating type. However, the literature identifies certain weaknesses inherent to flexible exchange rates. Without doubt, the main one is that if the exchange rate is determined by market forces, developing countries are at great risk of losing to the variable exchange rate as a nominal anchor of the economy. The former situation is the main reason that pure floating isn't the primary world exchange rate regime.

Once this research document theoretically analyzed the elements of the *tripod* of Taylor and, subsequently, evaluated them for the Mexican case in the past decade, we are finally able to make the final conclusion. The monetary policy of Mexico cannot be considered to be one that has put into practice the elements, tools, schemes, etc., for it to be called macroeconomic stabilization and, therefore, it cannot be assumed to be optimal. Here, optimum means good monetary policy, which, precisely, includes the three aspects that describe the Trinity proposed by Taylor. The various sectors of Mexican society, including those who do not sympathize with the monetary proposals reviewed herein, agree that the policy of price stability of the BANXICO has had some degree of success.

Also, in my opinion, consensus was detected regarding the observation that, in the case of Mexico, there is a rule by which the Mexican central bank guides the economy explicitly. By this method of proposal or suggestion, we should try to follow a behavior (rule) determined and, if possible, framed on the principle of Taylor to ensure the proper functioning of the same. At the same time, this would promote the reputation and credibility of the BANXICO, which is a current requirement for the implementation of monetary policy in any Monetary Institution in the world. I am convinced that the behavior that I sought during this investigation is there; so the question arises to detect it using other methodologies, instruments, and opportunities. This means it will need a new investigation that continues with the search for that component on the basis of the results obtained by this master's investigation.

REFERENCES

Ball, L. *"Policy rules for open economics"*, en *Monetary policy rules*, ed. J; University of Chicago Press: Taylor, 1999.

Banco de México. *Política monetaria e inflación: estadísticas*; México, 2012.

Banco de México. *Minuta número 1*, Reunión de la Junta de Gobierno del Banco de México, con motivo de la decisión de política monetaria anunciada el 21 de enero; 2011a.

Banco de México. *Minuta número 2*, Reunión de la Junta de Gobierno del Banco de México, con motivo de la decisión de política monetaria anunciada el 3 de marzo; 2011b.

Banco de México. *Minuta número 3*, Reunión de la Junta de Gobierno del Banco de México, con motivo de la decisión de política monetaria anunciada el 14 de abril; 2011c.

Banco de México. *Minuta número 4*, Reunión de la Junta de Gobierno del Banco de México, con motivo de la decisión de política monetaria anunciada el 27 de mayo; 2011d.

Banco de México. *Minuta número 5*, Reunión de la Junta de Gobierno del Banco de México, con motivo de la decisión de política monetaria anunciada el 8 de julio; 2011e.

Banco de México. *Minuta número 6*, Reunión de la Junta de Gobierno del Banco de México, con motivo de la decisión de política monetaria anunciada el 26 de agosto; 2011f.

Banco de México. *Minuta número 7*, Reunión de la Junta de Gobierno del Banco de México, con motivo de la decisión de política monetaria anunciada el 14 de octubre; 2011g.

Banco de México. *Minuta número 8*, Reunión de la Junta de Gobierno del Banco de México, con motivo de la decisión de política monetaria anunciada el 2 de diciembre; 2011h.

Banco de México. *Minuta número 9*, Reunión de la Junta de Gobierno del Banco de México, con motivo de la decisión de política monetaria anunciada el 20 de enero; 2012a.

Banco de México. *Minuta número 10*, Reunión de la Junta de Gobierno del Banco de México, con motivo de la decisión de política monetaria anunciada el 16 de marzo; 2012b.

Banco de México. *Minuta número 11*, Reunión de la Junta de Gobierno del Banco de México, con motivo de la decisión de política monetaria anunciada el 27 de abril; 2012c.

Banco de México. *Minuta número 12*, Reunión de la Junta de Gobierno del Banco de México, con motivo de la decisión de política monetaria anunciada el 8 de junio; 2012d.

Banco de México. *Minuta número 13*, Reunión de la Junta de Gobierno del Banco de México, con motivo de la decisión de política monetaria anunciada el 20 de julio; 2012e.

Barro, R.; D. Gordon. "Rules, discretion and reputation in a model of monetary policy." NBER Working Paper Series, Working Paper N° 1079, febrero, 1983.

Bernanke, B.; Mishkin, F. Inflation targeting: A new framework for monetary policy? *J. Econ. Perspect.* 1997, 11, 2. verano.

Bernanke, B.; Woodford, M.; Eds. *The Inflation-Targeting Debate*; The University of Chicago Press: Chicago, 2005.

Bernanke, B.; Laubach, T.; Mishkin, F.; Posen, A. *Inflation Targeting. Lessons from the International Experience*, 2ª edición ed.; Princeton University Press: New Jersey, 2001.

Bernanke, B. "Panel discussion", 28th Annual Policy Conference: Inflation Targeting: Prospects and Problems, Federal Reserve Bank of St. Louis, St. Louis, Mo, octubre, 2003.

Broaddus, A. "Macroeconomic principles and monetary policy", Federal Reserve Bank of Richmond. *Econ. Q.* 2004, 90(1), 1–9. invierno.

Calvo, G. *Monetary and Exchange Rate Policy for México*; University of Maryland: Maryland, 1997. mimeo, junio.

Calvo, G.; Mishkin, F. The mirage of exchange rate regimes for emerging market countries. *J. Econ. Perspect.* 2003, 17(4), 99–118. otoño.

Calvo, G.; Reinhart, C. Fear of floating. *Q. J. Econ.* 2002, 117(2), 379–408. mayo.

Capistrán, C.; Ibarra, R.; Ramos Francia, M. El traspaso de movimientos del tipo de cambio a los precios: un análisis para México. *El Trimestre Económico*. 2012, 79(4).

Chiquiar, D.; Noriega, E. A.; Ramos-Francia, M. A time series approach to test a change in inflation persistence: the Mexican experience. *Appl. Econ.* 2010, 42(24), 3067–3075.

Clarida, R.; Galí, J.; Gertler, M. Monetary policy rules in practice. Some international evidence. *Eur. Econ. Rev.* 1998, 42, 1033–1067.

Clarida, R.; Galí, J.; Gertler, M. The science of monetary policy: a new Keynesian perspective. *J. Econ. Lit.* 1999, 37(4), 1661–1707.

Clarida, R.; Galí, J.; Gertler, M. Monetary policy rules and macroeconomic stability: evidence and some theory. *Q. J. Econ.* 2000, 115(1), 147–180. febrero.

Clarida, R.; Galí, J.; Gertler, M. Optimal monetary policy in open vs. closed economies: an integrated approach. *Am. Econ. Rev.* 2001, 91(2), 248–252. mayo.

XXX. *Constitución Política de los Estados Unidos Mexicanos*, Constitución publicada en el *Diario Oficial de la Federación* el 5 de febrero de 1917. Última reforma publicada DOF 09-02-2012, Cámara de Diputados del H. Congreso de la Unión.

Contreras, H. La relevancia de la crítica de Lucas, *Carta de Políticas Públicas en México y en el Mundo,* año 4, núm. 34, junio-julio. Facultad de Economía, UNAM, 2003.

Contreras, H. Sobre las expectativas endógenas: el antiguo teorema de la telaraña y los nuevos libros de texto, *Economía Informa* núm 341, FE-UNAM, julio-agosto, 2006.

Cortés J. F. Una Estimación del traspaso de las variaciones en el tipo de cambio a los precios en México. *Banco de México*, Documento de investigación núm. 2013-02, marzo, 2013.

Financial Times. *Oil price fall disrupts Mexico's hedging and threatens spending*. Obtenido de The Financial Times, 2014.

El Financiero. La caída de los precios del petróleo: consecuencias para México. *El Financiero*, 2015. Disponible en: http://www.elfinanciero.com.mx/opinion/la-caida-de-los-precios-del-petroleo-consecuencias-para-mexico.html

Freund, J. *Estadística matemática con aplicaciones*; Prentice-Hall: México, 1990.

Milton, F. The role of monetary policy. *Am. Econ. Rev.* 1968, 58(1). , marzo.

Milton, F.; Savage, L. The utility analysis of choices involving risk. *J. Polit. Econ.* 1948, LVI(4). agosto.

Greene, W. *Análisis econométrico*; Prentice-Hall Hispanoamericana: Madrid, 1999.

Guerra de Luna, A.; Sánchez, M. Política monetaria y crédito neto: una lectura a través de los balances del Banco de México, Banco de México, II Congreso de Historia Económica, octubre, 2004.

Hilsenrath, J. Q&A: John Taylor on his rule and Fed's balance sheet, *The Wall Street journal*, octubre, 2009.

Judd, J. Inflation goals and credibility, Federal Reserve Bank of San Francisco, *Weekly Letter*, N° 95-19, mayo, 1995.

King, M. Whas has inflation targeting achieved? en Bernanke, Ben y Michael Woodford, eds, 2005.

Krugman, P. The madness of the monetary hawks (wonkish), *The New York Times*, octubre, 2009.

Kydland, F.; Prescott, E. Rules rather than discretion: the inconsistency of optimal plans. *J. Polit. Econ.* 1977, 85(3). , junio.

Lucas, R. Econometric policy evaluation: a critique. *Carnegie-Rochester Conference Series on Public Policy*. 1976, 1. enero.

Mishkin, F. Can inflation targeting work in emerging market countries? NBER working paper series, Massachusetts Avenue Cambridge, julio, 2004.

Modigliani, F. Deberíamos forzar las políticas de estabilización. *El trimestre económico*. 1985, lii(2), 206. México abril-junio.

Muth, J. Rational expectations and the theory of price movements. *Econometrica*. 1961, 29, 3. , julio.

Obstfeld, M.; Rogoff, K. The mirage of fixed exchange rates. *J. Econ. Perspect.* 1995. , otoño.

Orphanides, A. Historical monetary policy analysis and the Taylor rule. *J. Monet. Econ.* 2003, 50, 5. , julio.

Ortiz, G. Commentary: How should monetary policymakers react to the new challenges of global economic integration, *symposium*: Federal Reserve Bank of Kansas City, Jackson-Hole, Wyoming, agosto, 2000.

Ortiz, G. Inflation targeting, *a festschrift in honour of David Dodge*, Banco de Canadá, noviembre, 2008.

Ramos, M.; Torres, A. Reducing inflation through inflation targeting: the Mexican experience, Banco de México, documento de investigación N° 2005-01, julio, 2005.

Reinhart, C. The mirage of floating exchange rates. *Am. Econ. Rev.* 2000, 90, 2. , mayo.

Romero, J. ¿Es posible utilizar el tipo de cambio para hacer más competitiva la economía mexicana? *El Colegio de México*, Centro de Estudios Económicos, núm. X-2013, 2013.

Rubli, F. "La relevancia de las expectativas para los fenómenos monetarios", *Economía informa*, UNAM, núm. 341, julio-agosto, 2006.

Sen, A. Rational fools: a critique of the behavioral foundations of economic theory. *Philos. Public Aff.* 1977, 6(4). Princeton University, verano.

Sheffrin, S. *Expectativas racionales*; Alianza editorial: Madrid, 1996.

Svensson, L. The simplest test on inflation targeting credibility, NBER working paper N° 4604, Institute for International Economic Studies, Stockholm University, Stockholm, diciembre, 1993.

Svensson, L. Inflation forecast targeting: implementing and monitoring inflation targeting. *Eur. Econ. Rev.* 1997, 41.

Svensson, L. Open economy inflation targeting. *J. Int. Econ.* 2000, 50. , febrero.

Taylor, J. Discretion *versus* policy rules in practice, *Carnegie-Rochester Conference Series on Public Policy* núm. 39, 1993.

Taylor, J. *An historical analysis of monetary policy rules*; nber: Cambridge, 1999. , octubre.

Taylor, J. Recent developments in the use of monetary policy rules, Conferencia *Inflation targeting and monetary policies in emerging economies,* Banco Central de la República de Indonesia, julio, 2000.

Taylor, J. *Using monetary policy rules in emerging market economies*; Stanford University: 2000. , mimeo, diciembre.

Taylor, J. Low inflation, pass-through and the pricing power of firms. *Eur. Econ. Rev.* 2000, 44.

Taylor, J. The role of the exchange rate in monetary policy rules. *Am. Econ. Rev.* 2001, 91(2). , mayo.

Taylor, J. Increasing economic growth and stability in emerging markets. *Cato J.* 2003, 23(1). primavera-verano.

Taylor, J. Lessons learned from the implementation of inflation targeting, panel de discusión del ochenta aniversario del Banco de México, *Estabilidad y crecimiento económico: el papel del banco central,* noviembre, 2005.

Taylor, J. Taylor rule change will hurt Fed´s inflation fight: John Taylor, *Economics one,* 2009.

Taylor, J. Speaking of monetary policy rules. *Economics one,* octubre, 2009.

Taylor, J. *Getting Off Track: How Government Actions and Interventions Caused, Prolonged, and Worsened the Financial Crisis*; Hoover Institution Press: California, 2010. febrero.

Taylor, J. The Taylor rule does not say minus six percent. *Economics one,* septiembre, 2010.

Taylor, J. Lessons learned from Ben Bernanke's policy rule discussion at the senate. *Economics one,* marzo, 2011.

Taylor, J. References to policy rules in a speech by the Fed vice chair. *Economics one,* abril, 2012.

Taylor, J. The dangers of an interventionist Fed. *The Wall Street Journal,* marzo, 2012.

Taylor, J. *First principles: five keys to restoring America´s prosperity*, primera edición ed.; W.W. Norton & Company, Inc: Nueva York, 2012.

Taylor, J.; Williams, J. Simple and robust rules for monetary policy, en Benjamin Friedman y Michael Woodford, eds.: *Handbook of Monetary Eonomics,* abril, 2010.

Tobin, J. *Acumulación de activos y actividad económica*; Alianza Editorial: Madrid, 1980.

Torres, A. Un análisis de las tasas de interés en México a través de la metodología de reglas monetarias, *Documento de investigación núm.* 2002-11, Banco de México, diciembre, 2002.

Trehan, B. The credibility of inflation targeting, Federal Reserve Bank of San Francisco, *Weekly Letter*, N° 95-01, enero, 1995.

Yellen, J. The economic outlook and monetary policy, New York University, speech, abril, 2012.

Zárate, D. *El trípode de Taylor. La teoría y una aplicación al caso mexicano, 2001-2009.* Tesis de maestría. Facultad de Economía, Universidad Nacional Autónoma de México, 2010.

INDEX

For Product Safety Concerns and Information please contact our EU
representative GPSR@taylorandfrancis.com
Taylor & Francis Verlag GmbH, Kaufingerstraße 24, 80331 München, Germany

www.ingramcontent.com/pod-product-compliance
Ingram Content Group UK Ltd.
Pitfield, Milton Keynes, MK11 3LW, UK
UKHW021608240425
457818UK00018B/445